DON'T LIE TO ME

EVA RAE THOMAS MYSTERY - BOOK 1

WILLOW ROSE

Books by the Author

MYSTERY/THRILLER/HORROR NOVELS

- SORRY CAN'T SAVE YOU
- IN ONE FELL SWOOP
- UMBRELLA MAN
- BLACKBIRD FLY
- TO HELL IN A HANDBASKET
- EDWINA

HARRY HUNTER MYSTERY SERIES

- ALL THE GOOD GIRLS
- RUN GIRL RUN
- NO OTHER WAY
- NEVER WALK ALONE

MARY MILLS MYSTERY SERIES

- WHAT HURTS THE MOST
- YOU CAN RUN
- YOU CAN'T HIDE
- CAREFUL LITTLE EYES

EVA RAE THOMAS MYSTERY SERIES

- DON'T LIE TO ME
- WHAT YOU DID
- NEVER EVER
- SAY YOU LOVE ME
- LET ME GO
- IT'S NOT OVER

- Not Dead yet

- Thirteen, Fourteen…Little Boy Unseen
- Better Not Cry
- Ten Little Girls
- It Ends Here

HORROR SHORT-STORIES

- Mommy Dearest
- The Bird
- Better watch out
- Eenie, Meenie
- Rock-a-Bye Baby
- Nibble, Nibble, Crunch
- Humpty Dumpty
- Chain Letter

PARANORMAL SUSPENSE/ROMANCE NOVELS

- In Cold Blood
- The Surge
- Girl Divided

THE VAMPIRES OF SHADOW HILLS SERIES

- Flesh and Blood
- Blood and Fire
- Fire and Beauty
- Beauty and Beasts
- Beasts and Magic
- Magic and Witchcraft
- Witchcraft and War
- War and Order
- Order and Chaos
- Chaos and Courage

THE AFTERLIFE SERIES

- Beyond
- Serenity
- Endurance
- Courageous

THE WOLFBOY CHRONICLES

- A Gypsy Song
- I am WOLF

DAUGHTERS OF THE JAGUAR

- Savage
- Broken

The secret of change is to focus all of your energy, not on fighting the old, but on building the new.

Socrates

Prologue
CAMP SEMINOLE SPRINGS, FLORIDA

Prologue

"MOM. I don't want to stay at the camp for two weeks. I want to go home."

Sophie Williams choked back a sob as a tear left her right eye and rolled down her cheek. She had promised herself she wouldn't cry. She had promised herself she would complete this. But hearing her mother's voice on the phone had made her lose it. She couldn't hold it back anymore.

"I know, sweetie," her mother said. "I miss you too, baby. But it's only for two weeks. You'll be fine."

It was the first time Sophie had been away from her mother for this long. She was the one who had wanted to go when their scout leader had told them about the camp. Sophie had immediately known that she wanted to do this. But the other girls had been so mean on the bus ride there, and she had ended up sitting all alone without anyone to talk to. Now she felt lonely and, even though they weren't allowed to call home, she had snuck outside while they were eating dinner and walked back to her tent and found her phone in her backpack. She wanted to hear her mother's voice, just for a few seconds. But once she did, the tears piled up, and she felt so homesick it almost hurt.

"You'll be fine," her mother repeated. "It'll be over before you know it, and then you'll want to go again next year. I went through the same thing when I was your age."

"I'd much rather be at home and go surfing all summer," Sophie said.

"I know, baby, but you need to do other stuff too. You need to socialize with other children. Besides, you were the one who told me you wanted this, remember? You wanted to go to this camp with your new friends."

"But they're not my friends anymore," Sophie sighed.

"Really?" her mother said sounding tired. "That was fast."

Sophie knew her mother was disappointed. Sophie had never been good at making friends. That was why her mother suggested she join Girl Scouts. Sophie was homeschooled so she could focus on her competitive surfing on a daily basis and attend contests all over the country on the weekends. It was practically all she did in her life, and she loved it, but you didn't make any friends at surf contests. She would chat with other kids while waiting for her heat to start, yes, but in the end, they were competitors, and there was no room for friends. It was a lonely world for a twelve-year-old, especially since she was so young, yet better than most who were much older. Being a Girl Scout would be good for her, her mother had said. Plus, it would teach Sophie skills that would be beneficial later in life.

And Sophie had made friends. Marley and Grace had been her friends right from the beginning. But not anymore. Now they had turned their backs on her, for no apparent reason, and she was—once again—all alone.

"This is good for you," her mother said, and Sophie could tell she wanted to end the call. "Besides, it's only the first day. Sleep on it and then see if you don't feel different tomorrow when all the fun starts, okay?"

Sophie sighed. "Okay."

They hung up with an *I love you,* and Sophie put the phone back in her backpack. She glanced at her sleeping bag, then killed a mosquito that was sucking blood from her arm. Her legs were already covered in bug bites.

Prologue

SOPHIE RETURNED to the main building and found the others in the common area. Marley and Grace stuck their heads together as she walked past them and whispered, not even bothering to keep it so low that she couldn't hear every word they said.

"Where do you think she's been?"

"Probably out signing with a new sponsor."

"You think her underwear is sponsored?"

"Of course, it is. She can't even eat anything unless it's sponsored by the right company. When she poops, it comes out wearing that sponsor's name."

They laughed. Sophie gave them a look, then went to sit with someone else. She tried smiling at a girl named Britney, thinking maybe she could be her friend, but Britney rolled her eyes at her and turned her head away. Sophie exhaled and looked down at the floor while one of their leaders, Miss Michaela, explained what they were going to do for the next couple of days. The camp was right next to a spring and tomorrow they were supposed to go canoeing. Sophie had been looking forward to that part, but there had to be two girls in each canoe, and she knew none of them would choose her.

"They're just jealous," her mother had told her over and over again all through her childhood when things like this happened. It didn't make things any better that she was chosen as surfer of the year by Ron Jon's Surf Shop and they had her displayed on their billboards all over town. All the adults thought it was so cool, but the kids not so much. The neighborhood's girls had mocked her and told her she looked fat in the picture and that their parents would never allow them to be on display like that for child-abductors to see and get crazy ideas.

"Does your mom *want* you to be kidnapped?" A girl named Victoria who lived on her street had asked.

"Of course not," another girl named Alison had said. "She's planning on living off her money for the rest of her life. Sophie is her golden goose, remember?"

"That's right," Victoria had answered. "Now that your dad left, she's counting on you to provide for her. That's why she's pushing you so hard. At least that's what my mom says."

Sophie felt anger rise inside of her when thinking about those girls. What did they know about her life anyway?

"All right, next up is a bonfire," the leader said and clapped her hands.

"Yay," the girls exclaimed. "S'mores!"

"And scary stories!" Miss Michaela said, then looked at Sophie, who didn't get up when the others did. She walked to her and reached out her hand toward her.

"You can sit by me," she said with a wink.

Sophie felt relieved. She hated to constantly sit alone. She grabbed Miss Michaela's hand in hers, then got up.

"To tell you the truth. I don't really like scary stories either," she said smiling. "But don't tell anyone."

Sophie didn't mind the stories, but she was happy that

someone had finally spoken to her, so she simply nodded and held the hand tightly in hers.

At the bonfire, she stayed close to Miss Michaela, trying hard not to pay any attention to the other girls. As they sang songs and roasted marshmallows for s'mores, she thought about her mom and how she was going to call her in the morning and tell her she had made up her mind. Coming here had been a mistake. She wanted to go home. But she would at least finish the night. One night here could hardly hurt her.

Prologue

THEY HAD BARELY FINISHED their s'mores when a loud thunderclap surprised them, sounding almost like the sky cracked above them. Seconds later, the rain came down hard and soaked their clothes.

"Quick. Everyone go to your tents," Miss Michaela yelled.

Sophie ran to hers and rushed inside, then closed it up. The sound of the rain on top of it was comforting. She had slept in tents many times in her life when going to surf contests where they had to stay the weekend. It was the cheapest way for them to stay the night, and usually, they would find a local camp and set up the tent. None of her friends knew this about her, how much she had to go through to get to where she was, even sleep in tents on frozen ground in the winter time when they attended contests up north. But back then, her mother couldn't afford a hotel room like many of the other contestants, not when it was almost every weekend that they went somewhere. In the beginning, when she had started to surf, they had only done the local contests in central Florida, but as she got better, she was soon invited to bigger contests out of state, sometimes all the way in California, and that soon became very expensive for her mother.

Yes, she would win money, if she won, but that wasn't a given. Especially not in the beginning when she was so young and new to it.

It wasn't until she made the big leagues that the money started to come. That was when she got commercial contracts too, modeling for surf products and swimwear. That was where the money was.

Sophie grabbed her sleeping bag and opened it, then slid inside of it, thinking about her mother. They were really close since she was usually always with her wherever she went. Being away from her was a lot tougher than she had expected.

Sophie zipped up the sleeping bag and got comfortable while another tear escaped the corner of her eye. She wiped it away, then lay completely still, hoping for sleep to come quickly. She wanted this night to be over, so she could go home.

Some of the other girls were sharing tents, and she could hear them chattering and giggling as she tried to sleep. Seconds later, Miss Michaela shushed them, and they went quiet. Thinking she would finally be able to sleep, Sophie closed her eyes again and did a few of the breathing exercises that Coach Thomas had taught her to calm her down before a heat. She would always get a nervous stomach by the time they were about to enter the water, and it could throw her completely off balance. She loved surfing and the ocean, but not so much the fact that she had to constantly perform.

She enjoyed training for a competition way more than actually competing in it. But her mom was so proud of her for making it so far and for seeing her name and pictures in all the magazines and the local paper, that she never dared to say anything to her. But, if she was to be completely honest, all Sophie wanted was to surf for her own sake. Because it was fun. She didn't need the magazines or the fame or even to win. She liked it when she did but could be sick for days afterward if she didn't make it past the first round. Heck, even a quarterfinal wasn't enough to satisfy her mom anymore. She had to win, or it was the same as a failure.

"That's how real champions think," she always said.

Sleep, come on, sleep.

A hooting owl startled her, and her eyes popped wide open. Sophie stared into the ceiling of the tent, her heart pounding in her chest, then scolded herself for being such a wimp.

It was, after all, just an owl. She was out in nature, and there would be nature sounds. Sophie calmed herself down again using her breathing techniques, and soon her heart was beating normally again. She was about to close her eyes when the beam of a flashlight landed on the side of her tent.

Sophie gasped while her heartbeat ran amok. Seconds later, the beam disappeared.

Thinking it was probably just one of the leaders walking around to check on them, Sophie calmed herself down again. But now it was hard to fall asleep. Even harder than earlier. Sophie couldn't stop thinking that she had made a mistake in letting her mom talk her into staying the night. She should have insisted on going home tonight instead.

Sophie had barely managed to close her eyes again before she heard footsteps outside her tent. She laid completely still while listening to them come closer, then stared at the tent door, when the steps stopped right outside and lingered for a few seconds.

Maybe if you lay completely still, whoever is out there will go away.

But they didn't. The person outside bent down, zipped her tent open, then peeked inside. Before Sophie could even scream, this person grabbed her, then zipped up her sleeping bag until it covered her face completely. Sophie tried to scream and kick but was lifted off the ground and was soon moving swiftly through the night.

Chapter 1
THREE MONTHS LATER

"I'M CALLING DAD. He knows how to do it."

"No."

I stared at my twelve-year-old daughter, Christine. She was still holding her laptop in her arms. It had gotten a virus, and I had no idea how to fix it. The look in my eyes made her freeze.

"What do you mean, *no*?" Christine asked.

"Just what I said."

"But...?"

I shook my head while biting my lip. We'd had this conversation a lot lately, and it got to me every time.

"Dad's on his honeymoon, remember?" Alex, my six-year-old son, said from the other end of the kitchen counter. He was eating cereal with no milk because we had run out and I hadn't had time to buy more with all the unpacking I had to do. For some reason, my kids were like sponges when it came to milk, and no matter how much I bought, it was never enough. I couldn't believe how often I had to shop in order to keep up. After only a month as a full-time single mom, I was already quite overwhelmed.

It was Chad who had taken care of these things while the

kids were growing up. He had the privilege of being able to work from home for his insurance company, and so he was the one who had taken care of most of the housework for years. Needless to say, I was quite in over my head ever since he decided to leave me for a younger model and become a full-blown midlife crisis cliché. Kimmie had legs to up above her ears and hair blonder than platinum, not to mention a waist so slim it looked to be the size of my thigh. She also had a teenage son, and now Chad wanted to start a family with her. A new family. He had told me that a month ago, exactly to the date. I was still recovering from the enormous shock that had destroyed my world, not to mention our children's.

"It's not a honeymoon, sweetie," I said. "That would require them being married, which they are not."

"Yet," my fourteen-year-old daughter, Olivia, grumbled from the doorway.

"Hi, honey, are you hungry?" I asked, hoping to take the conversation elsewhere. She shook her head. I was worried about her since she hadn't talked much to any of us since her dad told us he was going to live at Kimmie's apartment from now on.

I still couldn't believe he would do this to us...throw fifteen years of marriage down the drain just like that. No...*I am sorry*, or *I hate to do this to you all*. There were simply five devastating words—said over the phone—that still rung in my head:

I am not coming home.

"But, Mo-om, what do I do about my computer?" Christine asked.

I stared at her, then at the boxes behind her. The moving truck had brought it all two days earlier, and I still hadn't unpacked half of them.

"I don't know," I said with a deep sigh. "Maybe I can take it to an Apple store next week?"

"Next week?" she whined. "Next week? I can't wait that long. I have math I need to do."

"Use my computer," I said. "You can access Google class-room from anywhere."

Christine made an annoyed almost gasping sound. I could tell by the look on her face that the thought of being without her computer for more than an hour was too much for her to handle, let alone several days. I knew the computer was her entire life, next to her phone, naturally, but she was on that darn thing all day when she wasn't in school. I had no idea what she did on it, but so far, I hadn't given it much thought either. I was in way over my head here, and what she was doing on her computer was the least of my problems.

"I won't do it," she said with an air of finality like there was nothing I could do or say that would make her accept the fact. This computer had to be fixed, now. That was the only solution she would take. But I just didn't have time for it right now. I was planning on unpacking all day and then hopefully getting some work done before going to bed.

"I am sorry, sweetie," I said. "But it's the best I got. I can do it first thing Monday morning, okay?"

My daughter grumbled loudly, then placed the computer on the counter.

"This would never have happened if dad was here," she said, then walked out the door.

I swallowed with the sensation of guilt fluttering in my stomach. I could have told her off; I could have said some-thing back to make her behave, but I didn't.

Because—let's face it—she was right.

Chapter 2

I HAD JUST HUNG up with the local pizza place when the doorbell rang. I opened the door and found my mom and dad on the other side. My mom held up a casserole for me.

"It's vegan," she said.

"Yum," I said without meaning it.

My mother looked at me victoriously. "I told your dad you didn't have time to cook."

I shrugged as they walked inside, and I closed the door behind them. "I ordered pizza. Does that count as cooking?"

My mom snorted. "Most certainly not. That's not food, Eva Rae Thomas. You really should start to think about what you eat."

She gave me a disapproving look, and I felt guilty once again. Yes, I had let myself go after the third child. And it hadn't been easy to eat healthy over the past few weeks with everything that had been going on. I did enjoy my comfort food. But so far, eating healthy wasn't exactly at the top of my long list of things to do. Right now, I was just surviving. I didn't care much what I looked like. I was just happy I wasn't in my PJs all day, crying over my failed marriage. That had to count for something, right?

"It's good to see you, Squirt," my dad said and kissed my cheek. *Squirt* had been his nickname for me since I was a child because I was the shortest in my family.

"The place looks better every time we come over."

I sighed comfortably. My dad. My private cheerleader and biggest fan. In his eyes, I could do nothing wrong, much to my mother's regret. She, on the other hand, believed I did everything wrong. I guess, between the two of them, you could say they landed on a healthy middle road. Maybe my dad just wanted to make up for what he saw my mom didn't give me. No matter what, I had spent most of my life trying to impress her, trying to get her to notice me and approve of me. Maybe even love me. Over the years, I had learned it was probably never going to happen.

"I was just finishing up another box in the kitchen," I said and guided them out there. My mother looked like she wasn't sure she could sit on the chairs and not get dirty.

"Sit down," I said, and they did, my mother brushing her seat off first.

"Can I get you something? A glass of wine?" I asked. "Beer?"

"I could do with a beer," my dad said.

He received a look from my mom, but I still served him one, knowing he wasn't allowed to have any at home. Not since my mom got on her health kick, ever since my dad was hospitalized with a colon disease that they had initially thought was cancer but turned out to be just an infection. Other than that, he was as strong as an ox and ran on the beach three times a week. But my mom only saw the disease and, over the past two years, she had been almost hysterical about what he ate or drank. I figured she had been terrified of losing him and scared of the loss of control she had suddenly felt, and therefore thought, if only she controlled what he ate, she could somehow get some stability in the chaos she felt inside. Emotions weren't easy for my mother and, over the years, I had learned to read between the lines to figure out how she really felt. I guess I never really felt like I knew her very well, but it had gotten better. I wanted it to. I wanted to be closer to them both, and that was why I had decided to move back to Cocoa Beach, where I was born and raised.

My dad drank from the beer with a satisfied expression on his face while my mom looked like I had served her lemon juice.

"We should probably eat that casserole while it's hot," she grumbled and got to her feet. "I'll set the table. Where are your plates?"

"In one of the brown boxes over there," I said and pointed at a stack of boxes leaning against the wall.

"You haven't even unpacked your plates?" she said. "You've been here a week?"

"I haven't gotten to it yet. Besides, the boxes only came two days ago."

"But still...? You certainly...you must have plates. What have you been eating from?" she asked, appalled.

"Pizza boxes, using napkins," I said with a shrug.

"Why, I have never. Why would you do that? You have children, Eva Rae Thomas. They need plates. They need things to be like they used to be. They need stability."

I bit my lip, knowing she wasn't actually talking about plates anymore. This was about something else. I knew she blamed me for Chad leaving us. Of course, she did. Why wouldn't she? She had never approved of me working and having a career.

"Yeah, well, you can't really control everything in life, can you? Sometimes you have to improvise, work with what you've got," I said, then walked to the counter and poured myself a glass of wine.

Chapter 3

DINNER WENT DECENT. My mom tried hard not to criticize me too much in front of the kids, which I could tell took quite an effort. Meanwhile, my dad hung out with Alex, and they talked about fire trucks, which was Alex's favorite subject to discuss. During the conversation, Alex got really loud and was almost yelling. My mom sent me a look.

"Alex, sweetie, remember to use your inside voice," I said, then added, "Grandma has a hangover and doesn't like loud noises."

"What's a hangover, Grandma?" Alex asked while my mom hissed at me.

"Eva Rae Thomas..." she turned and looked at my dad. "Jon, did you hear what she said?"

My dad and I locked eyes, and he struggled not to laugh. I chuckled, then grabbed another piece of pepperoni pizza. My mom gave me a disapproving look, but I ignored her. No one had touched her casserole except for herself. Even my dad had thrown himself at the pizza, and I was just happy that I had ordered the family size, so there was enough for everyone.

Alex grabbed my dad by the hand and pulled him up to

his room to show him all his books on fire trucks. I loved seeing the two of them together. It was great for Alex to have a male role model these days, and not many understood him. I had enrolled him in my old elementary school, Theodore Roosevelt Elementary School, as soon as we got here, but almost every day he had come home with notes from the teacher about his bad behavior. He was loud and refused to sit still, she said. It was never a problem before, so I told her it was probably all the new things going on in his life, plus the fact that his dad wasn't with him anymore. But as I said that to his teacher, I realized I actually didn't even know if it had been an issue earlier in his life. Chad and I had drifted apart over the past several years and hadn't talked much about those things. And the last thing I wanted was to call him in Greece and ask. I was determined to do this myself without his help. He was the one who had decided to pick up and leave. I was these children's mother. Of course, I could take care of them, even if it had to be alone.

"He's very loud, isn't he?" my mom said in almost a whisper. "And wild. Keep an eye on him all the time. You heard about that girl who was kidnapped recently, right?"

I had. How could I not? It was everywhere. It was all over the news constantly; they had put up posters downtown, and it was on the lips of everyone I met. A young girl, twelve years old, and a local surf-idol, the new Kelly Slater, if there ever was one, had gone missing from a Girl Scout camp three months ago. They had made several arrests but not found who took her yet, nor had they found her. As every day passed, it became less and less likely they'd find her alive. From my experience, it was very improbable that she would show up alive after so long. Still, the locals kept up their hope. Some even believed her father had taken her since there had been a dispute between the parents during their divorce. But her dad had been questioned, and there had been no sign that he might have taken her. Personally, I thought the local police seemed to have let him off a little easy since I would have gone harder on him, knowing kidnappings were most often done by family members, but it wasn't my case, and I was done with that part of my life.

"You need to keep him home till it's safe to go out," my mom continued. "Till they catch this guy. Especially with that wild nature of his. He might get himself in trouble, you know. He's trouble waiting to happen. I see it in his eyes. He's got that crazy look. I don't see it in other children. Lord knows, I never saw it in mine."

I shrugged. My mom never had boys; how would she know if he was wilder than others?

"He's a boy," I said. "They get wild sometimes. There's nothing wrong with him. He's just been through a lot lately."

"He sure has," she said and gave me another look.

"Okay, just say it, will you?" I said, sensing I had to stop with the wine now before I said something I would regret later on.

But my mom didn't. She never said anything directly to me. It was all between the lines and in her looks. I felt like screaming at her to just speak out. Just be honest.

"Say what?" she asked.

"You blame me for Chad leaving, don't you?" I swallowed the lump that was growing in my throat. "Because, of course, it's my fault, just like everything else in life. Ever since…that day. Was it also my fault dad got an infected colon, huh?"

She shook her head, then looked away.

I felt tears pressing behind my eyes and couldn't really hold them back anymore. A couple rolled down my cheeks. I felt so helpless, so lost. I had rented this strange house and had no idea if I would be able to afford to live in it. I didn't even know how to buy enough milk for my kids.

I stared at my mother, secretly praying she would stretch out her arms and just hold me. But she didn't. She spotted the tears, then sat there like she was paralyzed and looked at me before she finally rose to her feet.

"It's late. We should probably get home. Your dad needs his rest. Eight hours every night, per doctor's orders."

I can't even remember the last time you touched me, Mom. Can't you just give me a hug? Can't you just put your arm around me and tell me it'll be all right? That I am going to make it?

I looked after my mom as she walked up to Alex's room to get my dad. Seconds later, they had both left, and I was once again alone with my thoughts, the smell of vegan casserole lingering in my nostrils.

I wiped away my tears and finished my glass of wine, reminding myself I had decided not to feel sorry for myself in this, when Alex climbed into my lap and attacked me with a toy fire truck, making me laugh. I rustled his hair and kissed his forehead with a sniffle.

"We're going to be fine, aren't we?" I asked the child like he understood.

He gave me one of his endearing smiles. "I like it better here, Mom. You're home a lot more, and you don't yell as loud as Dad. Besides, you smell better."

"I sure do," I said, chuckling, hugging my son closer.

Chapter 4

THE LIGHT IS BRIGHT, almost too bright, and it hurts my eyes as I look up to the ceiling. I can't find my mom. Sydney is standing a few steps to my right, looking at a doll. Mom went down another aisle, and I don't know which one. Panic is about to erupt, but I don't dare to cry. My sister will only think I am a wimp.

"Are you lost, little girl?"

I look up. The man has no face in the light coming from behind him. He's wearing a green sweater. It's winter in Florida.

"No."

"Tsk. Tsk. Don't lie to me, little girl."

I shake my head. "I am not. Mommy's right over there."

He looks but can't see her. Neither can I, but I won't admit it. I don't want him to know that I don't know where my mom is. I feel scared. Sydney doesn't see anything. She keeps pulling Barbie dolls down from the shelves.

"Let me take you to her," the man says.

The faceless man grabs my arm and pulls. I freeze up. A lady passes with her cart, pushing it in front of her. The man smiles at her, then explains that his daughter is upset because he wouldn't get her a toy. The woman tells him her son just threw a fit because she *wouldn't give him candy, then continues, smiling at me. I want to scream, but I don't. Why don't I?*

I woke up with a start, bathed in sweat, gasping for air, heart thumping in my chest. It was still dark out, and my phone told me it was three in the morning. I couldn't sleep, so I got up, then walked down to the kitchen and grabbed a glass of water. In the dark window, I spotted my own reflection, then thought I saw the faceless man standing behind me, I gasped and pulled away. I closed my eyes for a few seconds, reminding myself it was nothing but a dream, then took in a few deep breaths before I once again opened my eyes and the man was gone.

I drank some more water while trying to get the dream out of my mind, but it didn't help. I then decided to go for a run. I found my running clothes and left the house, then ran down my street, where all the dark houses stared back at me.

With music blasting loudly in my ears, I ran through my new neighborhood where the houses had canals on both sides of them and boats in their backyards. Since I had grown up in Cocoa Beach, I still knew my way around town, and soon I was running down Minutemen Causeway toward downtown, panting loudly. It wasn't a very big town, and one that lived mostly off tourism and the notorious snowbirds that came down from up north and stayed the winter in their condos on the beach.

I ran past City Hall that also housed the police station, and the newly built fire station next to it that I had promised Alex we'd visit one day. I continued down to the beach and turned left, running toward the pier. As my feet hit the sand by the restaurant, Coconuts on the Beach, I began to run faster, trying to get rid of that grisly feeling the dream had left me with, trying to shake every emotion it had stirred up inside of me. You might say I was trying to run from it, but I wasn't doing a very good job. No matter how fast I went, no matter how much I pushed myself to my maximum, I couldn't get rid of it. Soon, I ran out of energy and had to stop, realizing I was very far from the shape I used to be in. The past few years had been a lot of desk work and, even though I tried my best to keep in shape, I had to admit I hadn't been doing enough. It was one of my promises to myself when I decided to leave my job and come down here, to get back in shape. Three children, too many pastries, and no exercise hadn't done much good for my body. To think I had once been the fastest in our unit.

You're forty-one, Eva Rae. You're not dead yet. You can still get it back.

I sat in the sand by the pier and stared out at the ocean so calm and beautiful. The moonlight was glittering on the surface, and I suddenly remembered all the evenings I had hung out here with my friends, drinking beer under the pier when we weren't allowed to yet, listening to Michael Jackson on cassette tapes, sitting around bonfires till the police chief came by and told us to get out of there, confiscating our beers. We knew he wouldn't tell our parents if we let him take the beers for him and his colleagues. That was how things worked back then. I wondered if kids still hung out under the pier at night. Cocoa Beach was the kind of town that didn't really change much, and right now, that was exactly what I needed. I'd had change enough for a lifetime over these past couple of weeks.

Chapter 5

I STAYED under the pier for a few more minutes, thinking about Chad and our life together, then cursed him for ruining everything, before once again ending up blaming myself because I hadn't taken proper care of what I had. It was the same circle of thoughts that would rush through me every night and even during the daytime.

Then I decided it was time to get back. Alex had suffered from nightmares a lot since his dad left, and I couldn't risk he would wake up and come to my room and not find me there. Luckily, his two older sisters were there in case it happened, and to my regret, he more often than not crept into Christine's bed instead of mine. I guess it had become a habit of his over the past several years since I had been away a lot on the job, and was often gone at night when they needed my assistance somewhere in the country.

I liked to tell myself I was saving lives, that I was doing something good, but I wasn't sure it had been worth it. Was it worth losing my marriage?

I got up, then brushed the sand off my behind, glanced once more across the ocean, then turned around and ran back, this time running a little slower, so I didn't exhaust myself quite as much. It took a little longer, but I felt better. When I walked up past the restaurant area by the beach, I thought I saw something and paused. A car was parked in the alley between Coconuts and Fat Kahunas, really close to the Hunkerdown Hideaway Bar. But all the restaurants and bars were closed now. A figure was by the car, just standing there, motionless. I stopped running and walked toward downtown, through the small square that had recently been renovated and closed to cars. I watched this figure in the alley as I walked by and felt like the figure was watching me as well, even though I couldn't see a face. I shivered even though it was eighty degrees out, thinking about the faceless man and almost felt the grab on my arm again. I walked faster, my eyes fixated on the figure that wasn't moving.

Are you lost, little girl?

I could still hear the faceless man's voice in my mind. My heart was pounding in my chest while I rushed past the alley, and soon I was running again. I was certain I heard footsteps behind me, but as I turned to look, no one was there. I ran as fast as I could down Minutemen Causeway and into my house, where I, wheezing and panting, threw myself on the floor after closing and locking the door thoroughly behind me.

You've gotta relax, Eva Rae. It was probably just someone going home after a night on the town. It was probably just some drunk.

I coughed while trying to calm my poor beating heart down. Meanwhile, I kept seeing the faceless man and feeling him grab my arm.

Don't lie to me, little girl. I noticed you were all alone.

When I caught my breath, I showered, then as my head hit the pillow once again, I finally managed to doze off. I got two hours of deep dreamless sleep before the door to my room slammed open, and Alex stormed inside, dressed in his full-blown fireman outfit that I had bought for Halloween, screaming FIRE, then pretending to rescue me.

"Alex, it's Sunday; please let me sleep, will you?" I moaned tiredly.

But it was too late. The boy yelled STOP, DROP, and ROLL, then started to pull my arm, trying to get me out of bed, then continued screaming DANGER, DANGER, swinging his plastic toy ax around, knocking down my lamp.

I sighed, then realized I might as well get up. I stumbled down the stairs, dreaming of coffee when I realized we were completely out. I looked at my phone. It was six o'clock. I wondered if anything in this sleepy town was open at this time, then decided something had to be. The gas station or Publix maybe?

Alex was screaming loudly and jumping on the furniture —the little I had since Chad had taken half of it—while saving imaginary people from an imaginary fire, and my head began to hurt. I knew I had to find coffee somehow. I grabbed my car keys and looked at my screaming son, real-izing I couldn't leave him here. He would tear the place apart before I made it back, and both his sisters were still sound asleep.

"Alex, we're going for a drive. Come."

"Yay, a drive! In the fire truck?" he exclaimed.

I smiled and nodded. "Yes. The big one. With the ladder. There's a fire downtown we need to put out."

"Then, we must hurry," he said, as he swung his ax and stormed out the front door, holding onto his fire helmet with one hand. "Come on, Mom!"

I trotted after him, feeling soreness in my legs from the run. What was I thinking? Going for a run in the middle of the night? It wasn't very like me. It had been a long time since I had last run like that, and I knew it was going to make me sore for days.

Getting in shape was harder than I had expected.

I strapped Alex into the back of my minivan, and we drove toward downtown, him wailing like a siren the entire way.

Chapter 6

AUBREY SIMMS YAWNED LOUDLY. She could barely see out of her eyes as she staggered around the corner, her two-year-old daughter pulling her arm while pointing and yelling behind her pacifier.

"Beach! Beach!"

Aubrey yawned again and followed her young, energetic daughter while dreaming about her bed. It was way too early to go to the beach if you asked her. The sun had barely risen yet. The sky was changing colors like it was preparing for its arrival, but it was still pretty dark out.

Going on a vacation with her daughter wasn't exactly how she had thought it would be. Naively, she had dreamt of long days at the beach, where she would lie in a chair working on a tan while her daughter played happily for hours in the shallow water or she would be swimming in the cool ocean while her daughter built sandcastles.

Boy, had she been wrong.

Just packing for a toddler had turned out to be quite an ordeal. Just the diapers alone had filled an entire suitcase, along with washcloths. And she had almost forgotten her special zip-up blanket that makes sure she isn't strangled at night. Not to mention the organic sunscreen and mosquito repellant, just to mention a few things.

But that wasn't the worst part. No, the packing she had done pretty fast. It was more the throwing up on the airplane, the diaper leaking accident in the Uber, and then there was the part about her getting up at five-thirty every morning begging to go to the beach. It would have been fine had the child only been able to entertain herself once they got down there, but, oh, no. Aubrey had to constantly observe her since otherwise she would run into the water on her own, or simply take off down the beach, running after birds or talking to people she didn't know. Aubrey usually wasn't overly protective, but she knew she had to keep an eye on the girl constantly, and it exhausted her immensely. There was no time for her to simply sit in a chair and work on her tan or even bathe comfortably in the ocean. There was a lot of crying and a lot of constant running from early morning to late at night. And if she didn't put her down for a nap during the day? Forget it. The rest of the day was completely destroyed with crying inconsolably and even screaming and throwing herself on the ground in a fit of rage when she didn't get her way.

It was true. She would never tell anyone, but Aubrey couldn't wait for this so-called vacation to be over, so she could go back to New York.

Now, they turned the corner toward the beach entrance next to the restaurant, where Aubrey had bought French fries for her daughter every day for lunch all week. She had done it even though it filled her with such a deep sense of guilt—just to make her sit still and be quiet for even just a few minutes so Aubrey could breathe.

As they turned the corner, Ani's hand slid out of her mother's, and she began to run.

"Beach! Beach!"

Realizing her daughter's hand was no longer in hers,

Aubrey rushed to catch up with her. Aubrey yanked her daughter's arm and pulled her back and was about to scold her for running away when she spotted something odd in the middle of the pavement. They had recently renovated the area and made it look nice.

"What's *dad*, mommy?" Ani said and pointed.

Aubrey shrugged. "Probably a homeless person," she said, knowing her daughter had no idea what a homeless person was. She stared at the sleeping bag that was zipped completely shut, but there was definitely someone inside of it.

"That's odd. Who sleeps in the middle of a street like that?"

Even for a drunk, this was an odd place to sleep. Yes, the area was closed to traffic, but still. There could be trucks coming to unload food or drinks for the restaurants or the bar next to them. They didn't open till ten o'clock, but people working there would most surely arrive soon. And in a few hours, the place would be crawling with tourists walking to the beach or the restaurants. Whoever it was could get hurt.

"Someone ought to do something," she mumbled, biting her lip and hoping it wouldn't have to be her. She looked around to see if anyone else was out, but the area was completely void of people. Even the Hunkerdown Hideaway on the corner was closed, and the drunks had left.

Aubrey looked down at her daughter, then shrugged. "Guess there's just us, then."

She walked to the sleeping bag, then knelt down next to it. Her daughter imitated her every move and sat next to her in the exact same manner, chewing on her pacifier, waiting to see what her mother was up to next, probably thinking it was all some fun game Mommy had come up with.

"Hello?" Aubrey said. "You can't sleep here."

The sleeping bag didn't move. It remained eerily still, and there was something about it that made the hairs rise on

Aubrey's neck. There was a stench that made her stomach churn.

Heart in her throat, Aubrey poked the person inside the sleeping bag. Still, no movement.

"Hello?"

Her daughter chewed her pacifier very pensively, then imitated her mother and poked the person too.

"Hello?"

Her daughter shook her head and threw out her arms.

"No one's home?"

Aubrey locked eyes with her daughter, then decided she'd have to take action. This person was in danger. If he was passed out drunk, there was no other way. She'd have to wake him up or move him to the side of the street. She grabbed the zipper and pulled it down.

With a gasp, she recoiled, and seeing her, Ani did the same. Next, Aubrey grabbed her daughter in her arms and ran down the street, both of them screaming.

Chapter 7

THANK GOD FOR GOOD BRAKES. I almost hit them with my car as they rushed into the street without looking where they were going. I stepped on the brakes, and the car skidded sideways and finally came to a halt.

Heart in my chest and panting in fear, I jumped out of the car.

"What the heck are you doing?"

The young mother and her young child in her arms both had terrified looks in their eyes. She tried to speak but didn't make much sense. She was gasping between the words.

"There...there's a...up there," the mother said, pointing. Her daughter was crying helplessly.

Thinking someone had tried to hurt them, I turned to look up the closed-off street, but they were all alone except for something lying on the pavement. The mother whimpered slightly, then caught her breath and spoke.

"There. Over there."

I stared at what she was pointing at. It looked like a sleeping bag.

"Stay here with my son, will you?" I asked. "I'm gonna have a look."

The woman nodded, then walked closer to my car that had ended up on the side of the road. Meanwhile, I approached the sleeping bag, bracing myself for whatever could be inside of it.

Was it some homeless person? Maybe he had died in his sleep? Maybe that was why she was so upset?

I decided that had to be it, then walked even closer, but as I did, my heart began to thump harder in my chest. As I moved closer, a face was being revealed from inside the sleeping bag that had been zipped down just enough for me to see it.

I clasped my mouth and gasped as the realization sank in. This was no homeless man who had drunk too much or even died in his sleep. No, this was a young girl, and I knew exactly who she was.

"Oh, dear God," I said, pressing back my tears.

Fumbling, I reached inside my pocket and found my phone. Then I dialed a number. It wasn't 911. Instead, I called the guy I knew would want to know about this first. The man I had watched on TV talk about the young surfer girl's disappearance over and over again. His name was Matt Miller, and he was a detective with the Cocoa Beach Police Department. He was also an old friend.

"Hello, Matt?"

"Who's this?" he asked, sounding sleepy and confused.

"It's Eva Rae."

A long pause.

"Eva Rae Thomas?" He suddenly sounded less tired. "Really?"

I bit my lip and looked at the dead girl in front of me. In the background, the woman and her child were still crying.

"Yes, really. I need you to come downtown. By Coconuts. I...I've found your girl."

He went quiet for a few seconds, then sighed profoundly.

"I'll be right there."

Chapter 8

IT TOOK him less than five minutes before he drove up and parked behind me. He rushed out and ran toward me. As I spotted him, my heart skipped a beat. I hadn't seen Matt in maybe twenty years, but he still looked the same. Older, yes, but that didn't make him any worse. Like many other men, he had gotten even more attractive with age. I didn't know how they did it.

His eyes locked with mine and he ran a hand through his thick hair that was brown but had been lightened by the sun and looked almost blond in places. It was a side effect of surfing and something a lot of the locals walked around with around here. Everyone surfed. Even the mayor and the city commissioners you would meet in the line-up in the water. I used to surf too as a child and teenager but hadn't been out there in many years. I often wondered if I still remembered how. I was a lot heavier now than I had been back then.

"You sure it's her?" he said, wrinkling his forehead.

"I have no doubt," I said.

He nodded heavily. "Okay."

He knelt next to the girl. I did the same. "The woman over

there thought it was a homeless person and was worried he would get hit by a truck or something, then went to take a look. She zipped it down and spotted the girl, then ran into the street, where I almost hit her with my car. I took one glance at her, then called you."

He swallowed. "Thank you."

Matt then grabbed the side of the bag and pulled it down to get a better look. As her face came completely into the light, I could tell his hand began to shake. Sobs emerged from his throat and, even though he tried to choke them back, he didn't succeed. Sobbing and gasping for breath, he pulled the zipper further down, so the girl's small body came into the light.

Then, he lost it. He sobbed and bent forward, crying, touching her long blonde hair between his fingers. "Oh, dear God, Sophie. What have they done to you?"

Knowing Cocoa Beach, I realized that Matt, of course, knew this girl very well and probably her parents too. I fought my tears as I wondered just how hard this was going to hit this small community, losing one of their own.

"Maybe we should not touch anything," I said, trying to remain professional. I wondered if this was the first time Matt had been called out to a dead child before. I had a feeling it was. I, on the other hand, had seen my fair share. I remembered each and every one of them and knew their faces. I knew what it was like. I knew it would never let you go again. I knew this one would never let Matt go either. She would haunt him for the rest of his days.

Matt didn't listen to me; instead, he zipped the zipper all the way down, so we could see the entire body, and that was when it got really creepy. It was so nasty that I almost threw up. Sophie's dead body wasn't complete. She had been dismembered.

With his face pale, Matt rose to his feet, took two steps to the side, then threw up on the pavement. The sound of him throwing up made me gag too, but I managed to remain in control, keeping all my emotions bottled up inside as life had taught me to.

Chapter 9
THEN

"WE NEED TO HAVE A TALK. Sit down, please."

The boy looked up at his father as he pointed to the couch. His sister was next to him and just as confused as he was.

"What's going on, Dad?" he asked.

"Just sit down, will you? Your mom is coming too."

The boy swallowed and did as his dad told him. He looked at his toys that were in a pile in the middle of the living room. He had forgotten to put them away when he was done playing. Was that why they needed to talk? They were mad at him, weren't they? Would they kick him out of the house? Or would they just yell? The boy didn't like the sensation deep in his stomach.

There had been a lot of yelling lately. Mostly by them, the adults, but also by him and his sister. None of them seemed to be getting along. It wasn't that he didn't love his sister, he really did. The day they brought her home from the hospital was the best day of his young life. He had wanted a sister for so long, longing for someone to play with. But lately, she had been so annoying he had to yell at her, just like his parents yelled at him. Otherwise, she would never learn, would she?

His mom entered the room. She looked so pale, it was

scary. The boy wondered if she was sick. Tommy from down the street's mom had been pale too for a long time, and then one day she hadn't gotten out of bed anymore. She was sick, his dad had told Tommy. And now he had to be quiet and let her sleep. And so she did. She slept and slept, Tommy said. Till one day when she didn't wake up anymore.

Was that what was what happening? Was Mommy sick? Was there a mommy sickness going around?

"We have something important to talk to you about," his mother said.

The boy's eyes grew wider. He could hear his own heartbeat and was about to cry, but knew he wasn't allowed to. Big boys like him didn't cry, they always told him. So, he had to keep it inside if he felt the need to. These days, it was only his baby sister who was allowed to cry. And she cried a lot. The boy was nothing like her. He could keep it in if he had to.

His dad took in a deep breath. The boy could tell he was angry by the way he was clenching his jaw. He could see it moving under the tight skin.

"Your mom and I..." he said, then looked briefly at the boy's momma before continuing. "We're..."

Then he stopped like he forgot the words, but luckily, the boy's mommy could remember them for him, so she took over.

"We're getting a divorce."

The word seemed so strange to him. Divorce? The boy had heard it before. Irene from his pre-school class had parents that were divorced, but he wasn't quite sure he knew what it meant. Apparently, it was something they had decided to get, so it wasn't a sickness. Because who would choose to get a sickness? The boy certainly wouldn't. He could still remember the time they had taken him to the hospital because he had a high fever. That wasn't very fun.

The boy's sister looked up at them, sucking her pacifier. The boy knew she certainly didn't understand what they were talking about. And neither did he. All he knew was that Irene sometimes came to class wearing the same clothes as the day before because her mom forgot to pack enough clothes. The boy didn't exactly understand why she had to pack any clothes for school but never dared to ask. Did this mean he had to wear the same clothes to school two days in a row? He didn't mind that much.

"Do you understand what we're telling you?" his mother asked.

The boy looked at his sister, who luckily shook her head, so he didn't have to admit he didn't.

"It means mommy and daddy won't live together anymore," she added, then looked at his dad, who had his head turned away while rubbing his hands against each other. The boy saw him clench his fist, then return to rubbing again before he turned his head back to look at them, his eyes almost glowing red.

"But...?" the boy asked, still confused. If they didn't live together, how would Daddy get food? They always ate Mommy's food at the round table together at six o'clock.

"It won't be too bad, kiddos," his dad said with a sniffle. "You'll be five days with your mom, then five days here with me."

"We've decided to split you evenly between us," his mom said. "That way you'll get just as much time with me as you get with your dad."

His father chuckled and poked the boy on the shoulder. "It'll be almost the same. Heck, you'll hardly even notice the difference."

The boy stared at his parents, wrinkling his forehead while wondering why it was so important for them to have this talk if it wasn't that big of a deal.

Chapter 10

I TOOK Alex home and woke up Olivia, then told her to keep an eye on him. She grumbled something about her wanting to sleep more, but I didn't listen. Alex jumped onto her bed and started to blabber on about the body they had found downtown.

"Wait, Mom?" she said and sat up on the bed. "You're working again?"

I shook my head. "Not really. Just helping out."

She looked confused. Her hair was standing out in all directions. She had cut it short a few months ago, and I thought it was cute on her. She had one of those thin fairy-like faces that made a haircut like that look good. She got most of her features from her father. Not like her sister. When her younger sister wanted the same haircut, I had to explain to her that it probably wouldn't have the same effect on her since she had my rounder face shape. It hadn't come out right, and she had ended up getting angry with me.

"Oh, okay," Olivia said.

"I'll be back again soon."

"Don't forget to bring back coffee," she yelled after me as I rushed out the door and into my minivan.

I drove back to the scene where a flock of spectators had now gathered. I spotted Matt fighting to keep people back. Photographers from local newspapers were there too now, and reporters were yelling their questions at them.

Matt looked like he could scream.

Our eyes locked and he let me come back in under the tape. "Boy, am I glad to have you back," he muttered.

"How does it look?" I asked.

He shrugged. "Still waiting for the techs. They should be here any minute now."

"Have you alerted the parents?" I asked.

He shook his head and scratched his stubble. "That was my next move."

"You might want to hurry up," I said and glanced at the crowd behind us. "It won't be long before the word is spread. The last thing you want is for them to be alerted through others."

Matt bit his lip. I remembered he used to do that as a child too when dealing with something difficult. A fond memory of him helping me learn how to ride a bike rushed through my mind.

"You could send someone else," I said. "If you don't want to leave the scene."

"No...it's not that. It needs to come from me. I've been on the case since the beginning and...I feel like I owe them."

"There's something I feel like I have to tell you," I said. "Last night, I went running down on the beach, and I passed by right here. I saw someone. A figure in the alley and a car. I can't help thinking that maybe..."

"Did you see who it was?"

I shook my head. "I couldn't see anything except that it was a white car. I couldn't see what type it was, but it was a four-door."

"SUV?"

"I don't think so, but I could be wrong. It was the middle of the night. It was after three o'clock, and it was very dark."

"But you saw someone here in the middle of the night? After the restaurants and bars had closed?"

I nodded. "It could have been anyone. At least that's what I thought. But now, I kind of think it might have been... whoever did this, whoever placed Sophie Williams here."

Matt nodded. "It might have been."

"Dang it," I said. "I knew I should have checked up on it instead of running away. I just...well, I wasn't armed or anything. I had this dream about...well, it doesn't really matter, but I couldn't get rid of this feeling. It brought me right back."

Matt nodded. "That's only natural. I'll need to..."

He didn't get to finish the sentence before there was a loud scream coming from the back of the crowd. We both turned to look simultaneously. A woman elbowed her way through. Her screams made the crowd disperse and create a path for her. As I saw her face and heard her shrieks of horror, I recognized her from TV.

Sophie's mother.

"SOPHIE!"

Matt approached her. "Ma'am..."

But she didn't listen. She pushed him aside, then ran to the sleeping bag, wailing.

"Sophie! No! Sophie, no!"

Matt glanced at me, and I knew he needed my assistance, so I followed him toward the woman.

"Mrs. Williams, Jenna..."

But the woman didn't budge. She stood like she was paralyzed and stared at the dead body, her torso shaking.

"Please," she said and fell to her knees. "Please...God...no!"

It was hard to hold my tears back. I took a couple of deep

breaths while Matt looked at me for help. I signaled for him to stay back and let the woman grieve.

Jenna Williams did. She cried and sobbed and then, as she had no more tears, she turned to face Matt.

"You knew about this. Why didn't you tell me?" she hissed, tears streaming across her cheeks.

"Jenna, I...I..." Matt said.

"Who?" Jenna said. "Who did this? Why? Why, Matt?"

"I...We don't know," Matt said.

"You don't know? You don't know?" Jenna Williams said, her voice shrill and high-pitched. She looked at Matt for an explanation, but none came. He had no words.

"Yet," I said stepping forward. I could tell Matt was in over his head, so I reached out my hand. "Hello, Mrs. Williams. Eva Rae Thomas, FBI. If you come with me, I'll try and answer your questions to the best of my knowledge."

Chapter 11

"I OWE YOU. BIG TIME."

It was past noon when Matt came up to me. His hair was standing out in all directions, and I swear I could see a couple of grays I hadn't seen earlier. I had been talking to Jenna Williams for about an hour, explaining to her what would happen next, that they would take her body in for an autopsy and then we would know more. I also assured her that Matt and his colleagues would do everything in their power to find whoever had hurt her daughter and make sure that justice was done. Then, after trying to answer her many questions as best I could, I hugged her, then sent her off with a couple of officers who wanted to take her statement.

I smiled at Matt. "You sure do."

He handed me a cup of coffee, and we sat on a bench that leaned up against the oyster bar.

"You're gonna need to do more than just bring me coffee," I said, "but I'll take it. For now."

He chuckled, and we sipped our coffees for a few seconds, not saying anything. The place was crawling with crime scene techs, and Matt had called in all his colleagues to ensure that the scene remained clear of people. The local NEWS13 was doing a live segment a few yards away, the reporter trying to explain what had happened. Matt had given them a statement, and that seemed to satisfy the vultures for a little while at least. There were still so many unanswered questions, and I knew from experience that they would be back.

"So...I heard from Melissa that you were back," he said. "I ran into her outside of Publix two days ago."

Melissa was another of my old friends. I had known her and Dawn since we went to pre-school. I hadn't seen any of them yet. I had planned to but kept postponing it, telling myself I wanted to be unpacked first. But the fact was, I was scared to see them again. Were they still my friends after all these years? I hadn't exactly been good at keeping in contact with them.

"So, what do you make of it?" Matt asked and nodded toward the scene where the techs were still securing evidence.

I shrugged. "Hard to say before we have anything from them."

"I've never seen anything like this," he said.

"You don't say?"

He gave me a look. I shook my head. "Sorry, sarcasm is my thing now. Comes with the job...and growing up with my mother, I guess. So...how long have you been working homicide?" I asked.

"Couple of years."

"And homicide also works kidnappings?" I asked.

He shrugged. "We do everything, I guess. We've never really had any kidnappings around here before...or at least not since...you know..."

I felt a knot in my throat. "Of course."

He sent me a sympathetic look, then stared down at his coffee as he sensed I didn't want to talk about it.

"You know how it is in this town and with the Cocoa Beach Police Department. Everyone pitches in. We do a little of everything. We help tourists who had their phones or wallets stolen, we drive home drunks, remove gators if they get too close to people, take care of traffic issues downtown, and keep an eye on the citizens during Friday-fest. We did have this guy recently who was conning old ladies by selling them stuff for their pools that wasn't actually his. I got him nailed down. But that's about it. Oh, yeah and then there was that bar fight last year where a man was stabbed. I got that guy too."

"Looks like you've got quite the track record here."

"I'm their shining star," he grinned.

I bobbed my head, realizing that nothing had truly changed in twenty years around here. A few new restaurants had popped up while others were gone, but that was about it.

"So..." he said. "What brings you back here? The Hoover building not big enough for you anymore?"

I chuckled and sipped my coffee. "Something like that."

"Where's Chad?" he asked, saying his name like he was annoyed by just the mere sound of it. "That's his name, right? The guy you ran off with?"

"I didn't run off with him," I said. "I met him in college, and we got married."

He sipped his coffee. "So, where is he now?"

"Greece," I said. "Last I heard."

He widened his eyes. "Oh."

"Yeah, you can say that again," I said. "With some girl named Kimmie."

Matt nodded. "I see. And the kids?"

"They're here with me." I gave him a look. "Hey, you already knew all this, didn't you? Nothing gets past you in this town."

He chuckled and nodded. "Just wanted to hear it from your own lips."

Chapter 12

IT WAS early afternoon before I finally made it back home, holding a package of coffee from Wahoo Coffee in my hand and a gallon of milk from Publix in the other. I could hear their loud voices as soon as I opened the door to the car. I rushed to the front door and walked inside.

"What is going on here?"

Christine looked at me, and so did Alex. She had her arm wrapped around him in a tight grip.

"Mo-om," she said and let go of him. He pushed himself free, then turned around and kicked her shin.

"Ouch, you little…" she said and ran after him.

"STOP!" I yelled. They both froze in place.

I slammed the door shut behind me. I stared at Christine. "Why are you hurting your brother?"

She made an annoyed sound, making sure I understood how unfair this was. "He…he started it."

"That's not what I asked," I said.

Christine gave me a look. I could tell she was looking for the right words to say.

"I can't believe you," I said. "When I'm not home, I expect

you and your sister to look after your brother, and this is what I come home to?"

"But...but he..."

"You're the big sister, Christine. This was an emergency situation today, and I had to be somewhere else. I need to know that I can count on you in emergency situations. Now, where's your sister?"

"Upstairs," Christine said. "Doing her homework."

"Okay, then when she's not available, you need to be the responsible one, okay?"

Christine stared at me, her nostrils flaring. "But..."

"I can't do this right now," I said, exhausted. "Just for once, say, okay, Mom, will you?"

Christine bobbed her head. "Okay."

"Thank you." I looked at Alex and held up the milk. "Now, who wants cereal?"

He beamed with happiness. "Me, me! I'm starving."

I chuckled and looked at Christine. "How about you? You want a little late breakfast?"

Christine shook her head, turned around, and stormed up the stairs. I looked after her for a few seconds, then reminded myself that she was a pre-teen and it would pass. I returned to the kitchen and poured Alex some Cheerios with milk. He ate greedily and told me all the games he was planning on playing for the rest of the day, and I got exhausted just listening to it.

I glanced at the living room. It looked like a bomb had gone off in there. Toys were everywhere. The house was a mess. I looked at the clock, then sighed. I had hoped I would be able to work a little today, but I also had to unpack more boxes.

Gosh, I loathed moving.

Chapter 13

I WAS DOING GREAT. I really was. Two more boxes had been emptied, and their contents had found their place in my new small house. It was beginning to look like a real home.

Then I found the box with our photo albums. That's when everything broke down.

I knelt next to it and pulled them out. Most people didn't do albums anymore. I hadn't been one of them. As the kids grew up, I had made sure to have books made with all our photos, and now I was staring at myself sitting on a beach in Italy on our honeymoon. The sight of my happy and tanned self next to Chad brought tears to my eyes, and I put the album aside. But only to pull out the one from our vacation in New Orleans with our two girls, before Alex was even a thought. I couldn't help myself; I had to look through them. I couldn't believe how happy we all seemed back then...how much I was smiling. The girls were only three and five years old and the cutest things ever. In each and every picture, I beamed with pride and glanced lovingly at Chad by my side.

Had life ever been that happy? I could hardly remember feeling that way.

It wasn't just albums in the box; it was also all the photos that we had hanging on the wall by the staircase in our old house back in D.C., the children's childhood home. All those wonderful photos I had looked at every day when coming home late at night or sneaking out early in the morning to go off to work. Or at least I ought to have stopped and looked at them, but I never recalled doing so. I was so busy rushing on with my career that I had hardly noticed them in the end; the photos and those in them.

I sunk to the carpet in the living room. Leaning my back against the wall, I stared at this weird room I was in now, not knowing what I was even doing there.

"STRANGER DANGER!"

My heart literally skipped a beat. Alex jumped out in front of me, holding a lightsaber, screaming the words he had learned in school recently and that he couldn't stop yelling at me every chance he got to scare me. I had explained to him that Stranger Danger was something you yelled if a stranger came up to you and tried to grab you, not something you yelled at people to scare them and give them a heart attack. It was a silly saying, I had always thought. It only told the kids to fear strangers, that all people they knew were safe, when, in fact, most abductions were made by people the child knew.

"Alex!" I said. "You can't do this to me. It has to stop."

The boy gave me a confused look, then swung the lightsaber at me like he was killing me. I pretended to die and made gurgling sounds. The boy laughed victoriously, turned around and left. A few seconds later, I heard him yell the words once again, and one of his sisters screamed at me from upstairs.

"MO-O-OM!"

I exhaled. I wondered if I had any more wine, then cursed myself for not buying more while I was at Publix. I wasn't very good at planning ahead. I walked to the kitchen and found the empty bottle from the night before, then sighed.

Alex yelled something from upstairs, and I turned around

with the intention of going up there and yelling at them when there was a knock at my front door. I walked to open it.

Outside stood Melissa and Dawn. Melissa smiled and held up a bottle in her hand.

"We brought wine."

"And a pie," Dawn said. "To welcome you back."

Chapter 14

"I MEANT TO CALL; I really did," I said as we sat down in the kitchen. Melissa found three glasses and started to pour the wine.

"We know," Dawn said and found the plastic forks and plates. She cut out a piece of the key lime pie for each of us and handed me a plate.

"I feel terrible," I said.

Dawn grabbed my arm. She looked me in the eyes. "Stop it. It's okay. You've been through hell. You're here now. And so are we. The rest is water under the bridge."

I swallowed, remembering how much I had missed those two. Back in high school, we had been inseparable. We had shared everything. Then I went off to college, and we lost contact, even though we tried to keep it.

Both Melissa and Dawn had attended local colleges and stayed in town like most people did. Meanwhile, I had run away as fast as I could.

Melissa handed me a glass of wine, then smiled.

"Now, you tell us everything. From the beginning."

I took in a deep breath, then sipped my wine. I told them

everything. Beginning with the day a month ago when I had come home from work and found the kids home alone.

"At first, I thought he had probably just popped out for pizza or maybe some wine," I said. "So, I walked to my bedroom and got into some more comfortable clothes and, when I opened the walk-in closet, half of it was empty. His side was nothing but empty hangers. That's when panic set in. I ran to the kids' rooms, and they were just hanging out. They had no idea where their dad was. He had been there a few hours earlier, Christine told me. She thought he had passed out in front of the TV.

"So, he didn't even say goodbye?" Dawn asked, almost dropping the piece of pie on her fork.

I shook my head. "He had just left. I called him, but he didn't pick up. Needless to say, I didn't sleep at all that night. The next morning, he finally picked up. He was at Kimmie's, he said. He lived there now. I didn't even know who Kimmie was. Apparently, he had been seeing her for quite some time now. More than a year. They had met at Olivia's school play, where they were both volunteering, doing the props together. Her son went to Olivia's school. He was done, he said. With me, with our life together, with everything."

"Oh, the bastard," Melissa said and sipped her wine, fuming. "And to think that you supported him all that time. He never worked, did he?"

"I made enough money, so he didn't need to work at all, but he wanted to. So, he started selling health insurance out of the house. But in the beginning, we had a deal. I was to work, and he would stay at home, at least while the kids were young. He was the one who suggested it be that way, and now, that was why he was leaving me. He didn't feel appreciated, he said. Kimmie appreciated him."

"But you got to keep the kids?" Melissa asked, her big brown eyes staring at me.

I shrugged. "Nothing's settled yet. So far, he and Kimmie

went on a trip to Greece. I'm guessing we'll deal with it when he comes back. I told him I wanted the kids, that he was the one who left, so he wasn't getting them."

"But…you moved down here?" Dawn asked. "Why?"

"I needed to get away. I couldn't stay at that house; I couldn't stay in the job. I tried for the first few weeks, but it didn't work. I was too much of a mess. The kids and I were constantly fighting, and I couldn't handle both them and my job. It was too much. I wanted to come back to be close to my family, to start over, fresh. Chad said it was okay. I get the feeling that he doesn't really want the kids anymore. I don't know how you can just turn it off like that, but it feels like he has. I fear that he's going to start a new family with that Kimmie character and forget all about us, forget about his children."

"Oh, the bastard," Melissa repeated.

"So, you don't work for the FBI anymore?" Dawn asked, sounding almost disappointed.

"Nope. I quit," I said and sipped more wine. "I needed a break."

"But why? You had this big career and everything? We were so proud of you," Dawn said.

That made me smile. "I don't know if there really is much to be proud of."

"Nothing to be proud of?" Melissa gaped. "What are you talking about? You made a difference in that job. Remember when you solved that case with that guy who had kept children in his house for years and raped them and made those awful videos? I think you made quite a difference to them."

"And to all the other children he will never touch in the future," Dawn added. "Don't think we didn't hear about your accomplishments down here."

I felt mushy. Maybe it was the wine. I stared at them and their pride-filled eyes looking back at me. They seriously saw me as some hero? The case they mentioned was so many years ago. How could I tell them I had screwed up? That I had messed up a case and lost a child in the process?

I decided not to.

"Aw, you guys."

"So, what are you going to do now?" Dawn asked. "You can't just be a full-time mom, can you?"

"Hey," Melissa complained, "I'm a full-time mom."

Dawn pointed at me. "Her. I'm talking about her. It's Eva Rae Thomas. She couldn't sit still if her life depended on it."

"She's right. I am not going to be a full-time mom," I said. "Or, that is, I am, but I am also doing something else. I'm writing another book."

"Uhhh, that sounds awesome. What's it about?" Melissa said.

"Serial killers. I signed a contract with a big publishing house to write about the minds of some of the most notorious serial killers in US history. You know, seen from a profiler's perspective."

"Nice," Dawn said.

I shrugged and looked at the boxes still surrounding us. "If I can ever get to it. Between unpacking and taking care of the kids, I don't really have much time."

"It'll come," Melissa said. "Speaking of gruesome murders, did you hear about Jenna's daughter?"

I nodded. Dawn did too. "Awful," she said. "Can you imagine? Going through a divorce and then this? She must be devastated. That girl was her entire life. She homeschooled her and everything, so she could focus on her surfing. Jenna took her to competitions every freakin' weekend."

"And she was good. We haven't seen anyone like her since Kelly," Melissa said. "At least that's what they say. I have never surfed myself, so I really don't know much about it."

"It's truly awful," Dawn said. "I mean, who would want to harm Sophie Williams? We all freakin' loved her. She could draw quite the crowd when she surfed by the pier—

such a talent. It's a shame. It's going to crush so many around here."

"I feel for her mother," Melissa said. "Can you imagine losing your daughter like that? I hope they catch the bastard and do the same to him. But until then, I, for one, am keeping a close eye on my children. I bet the dad did it, though."

"Why do you say that?" I asked.

"They went through a custody battle. But not because of the girl. He wanted part of her money. You know her sponsorships, her prize money and so on. That girl was made of pure gold. She's made a ton of commercials and has modeled for all kinds of stuff, like those expensive watches and sports drinks. They say the girl is good for almost five hundred thousand already, and they predicted she would go on to make millions once she got a little older. He wasn't going to let all that money go without a fight. It got ugly and was in all the papers. The media loved the stuff. They were all over it."

"But why would he kill her if he wanted the money?" I asked. "She's not going to make him anything now."

"To get back at his ex? So she wouldn't get anything either. I don't know. You're the expert here. You tell me."

"You were there, weren't you?" Dawn asked. "When she was found. Mrs. Hannigan from down my street said she saw you...and Matt."

Melissa gave me a look. "You were hanging out with Matt?"

I shook my head. "Not exactly hanging out. I happened to be in the area when the woman who found her came running into the street. I actually almost hit her with my car. Then I called Matt. I knew he was on the case. That's all there is to that story."

"I bet you and Matt are going to solve the case together," Dawn said.

"And then live happily ever after," Melissa added. They laughed and clinked glasses.

"Dream on," I said. "I am not exactly looking to hook up with anyone right now. I'm in the middle of a divorce, in case you didn't notice. Kind of brokenhearted right now."

"It's always been you two," Melissa said, completely ignoring what I had said. "Remember how he used to run after you in pre-school? He got himself in so much trouble because he kissed you once. The teachers had to have his parents come in and everything."

"I don't remember that," I said.

"Well, you were four," Melissa said. "I just have a freakishly good memory. At least when it comes to stuff like this. He also gave you a ring once, I recall. On the playground at the school."

"That, I remember," I said. "I also remember giving it back to him in fifth grade because I thought he had grown to be rude and annoying."

"But you dated in high school. You can't have forgotten that," Dawn said.

I sighed and leaned back in my chair. "Only a few times. We were best friends. I didn't want to ruin that."

"I think he saved himself for you. Waited for you to come back," Melissa said.

"You're such a romantic," Dawn said. "He just couldn't find anyone as good as her. You ruined him."

"Either way, he's single and has loved you forever. It doesn't get any more romantic than that," Melissa said, her eyes swimming.

I threw a spoonful of the whipped cream at her, and she ducked. Then we laughed. Her smile created dimples in her round cheeks. Hearing them both laugh like that made me remember how much I loved hanging out with them. Being back with them felt more like home than D.C. ever did for fifteen years.

Chapter 15

WE TALKED FOR HOURS. I called for pizza, and we ate with the children while laughing loudly and sharing fond memories and catching me up on everyone in town. I quickly learned that Melissa's husband, Steve, had been diagnosed with MS a couple of years ago, and was fighting the symptoms that grew more and more persistent each day. Meanwhile, Dawn still hadn't settled down with anyone yet.

There was a honk from a car outside, and Dawn's face lit up. "That's Phillip."

"Phillip?" I asked.

"Her latest boyfriend," Melissa said with a deep sigh.

"What?" Dawn asked. "He's cute."

"He's a firefighter," Melissa said as Dawn rushed to the door and waved for him to come in.

"He's more than that," Dawn said. "He's the captain. Here he comes."

Melissa rolled her eyes. Phillip came to the door, and Dawn grabbed his hand. "I want you to meet someone," she said.

Phillip smiled and approached me, holding out his hand. "You must be Eva Rae Thomas."

"I am."

"I live right down the street from you. Two houses down. I've heard a lot about you," he said.

"Oh, really?"

"Yeah, well, people talk; you know."

"They sure do," I said.

"Phillip came to town two years ago from Daytona Beach," Dawn said, still holding his hand in hers.

"I see, and how do you find it here?" I asked.

He smiled. "Hot and humid. Listen, we should get going. It's late, and I have to be at the station early tomorrow."

Dawn gave me a hug and told me how happy she was that I was back before they left. Melissa shook her head.

"What? You don't like him?" I asked.

"He's too perfect; you know?"

I chuckled. "How can anyone be too perfect?"

"He just is. You should see his house. Everything is so neat. And clean. Dawn says he cleans all the time when he's not working."

"Does he have any children?" I asked and grabbed another piece of the pie that Dawn had left behind.

"A daughter," she said. "Recently divorced. According to Dawn, he is perfect. But a guy like him is bound to have a few skeletons in his closet, am I right? Nobody is that perfect. I mean, did you see his body? You can practically count the muscles through his shirt. It's too much."

"I take it you're not a fan of them dating," I said and poured us some more wine. The kids were too quiet upstairs, and I had to get Alex to bed soon but hanging out with my friends made me feel better than I had in a very long time. Even before Chad told me he was leaving me. I was beginning to realize I hadn't been happy for years. It wasn't just the divorce; this had started way earlier.

"I don't know," Melissa said. "I'm happy for her, but I just hope he treats her right, you know? She has a way of picking them."

I bit my lip, remembering her with Tim who she had dated right after high school. I also remembered the bruises she was trying covering up with heavy make-up when I met up with her when coming back for winter break from college. My guess was he wasn't the only one she had found who had been abusive to her. Just like her dad had been when we were growing up.

"She had cancer, you know?"

I shook my head, almost choking on my wine. "No. I didn't."

"Ovaries," she said. "Had it all removed down there. Can never have children."

I sighed and leaned back in my chair. My friends had been through so much while I had been gone, and I had no idea. They had needed me, and I hadn't been there for them. Just like I hadn't been there for my family. I had been busy saving others, yes, but at what cost?

As I said goodbye to Melissa, who needed to get home to the kids and Steve, I couldn't stop thinking about that poor girl Sophie and her mother, Jenna. I wondered if Matt would get any sleep at all tonight. I, for one, knew the images of the poor girl lying in that sleeping bag were going to haunt me for a very long time.

Chapter 16

"I DON'T WANT to wear that!"

Alex growled and pulled off his pants that I had just helped him put on.

"No, Alex," I said, then looked at the clock on the stove. We only had ten minutes before the bus would be here. We had overslept, and I hadn't made lunches yet.

Olivia came rushing down the stairs, then grabbed the milk and poured some on a bowl of cereal. She had head-phones in her ears, and they were playing very loudly while she ate and put on shoes at the same time.

"Why are you up already?" I asked. She stared at me like she didn't understand. I signaled for her to pull out the head-phones, then repeated the question.

"I have A-OK club today before school," she growled at me. "I told you Friday that I joined this club for volunteer hours. You should know this by now, Mom."

I stared at her but didn't want to ask what A-OK club was since I had a feeling I had asked before.

"Okay," I said. "And what time are you out today?"

Olivia sighed deeply, then grabbed her backpack. "I have volleyball practice. It's Monday, Mom. You know this."

"Volleyball, check. I got it."

Olivia stared at me.

"What?"

"Lunch?" she said.

"Shoot!" I replied. "I'll give you money."

Olivia rolled her eyes and walked away. "Never mind. I already have money."

Then she left. My eyes fell on Alex standing by the fridge. He had no pants on. They were lying on the floor in front of him.

"Alex!"

"It's Monday," his sister said coming down the stairs. She picked up his pants and folded them. "On Mondays, he always wears his *Star Wars* pants."

"What?" I asked.

Christine shrugged. "It's been like that since Kindergarten. You really should know this, Mom. Dad would always make sure his pants were washed and ready for him."

"And since I haven't done the laundry this weekend, they aren't. I see."

"I want my pants," Alex yelled and stomped his feet. I sighed deeply. "Well, you can't have them. They're dirty."

On that response, Alex threw himself on the floor in a regular fit of rage. I felt so worn out, so exhausted, I didn't know what to do. Christine sighed, then disappeared up the stairs. She came down holding his red *Star Wars* pants featuring Darth Vader on the right leg and Chewbacca on the left.

"Here. Wear them even if they stink," she said and threw the pants at the boy.

Alex grabbed them happily and put them on. I looked at my daughter with gratefulness. She grabbed the milk jug standing on the counter, then shook it.

"Really? We're out of milk...again?"

I stared at her. "What? How is that possible? How are we

out of milk already? I just bought this yesterday? How did you kids drink a gallon of milk in less than twenty-four hours?"

Christine sighed. "Really, Mom? It's our fault now? Maybe next time you should buy some more."

I exhaled. The girl was right. I should get better at planning ahead.

"All right. I'll buy two gallons today. Until then, can you just eat it with no milk, please? After that, I'll drive you both to school since I just saw the bus drive past our house."

Chapter 17

I DIDN'T GO BACK HOME after dropping off the kids. Instead, I continued through my neighborhood and stopped at a house two streets down. The Williams were new in town, or at least they hadn't been there back when I used to live here. But I knew they had moved into old Mrs. Robinson's house after she died ten years ago.

I walked up the driveway holding a box of chocolates I had bought at the gas station in my hand. I rang the doorbell.

It took a little while before Jenna opened the door. Her eyes were bulging and red. She looked like she hadn't slept in a year. I smiled compassionately, then handed her the chocolates.

"I thought I had to at least bring something."

"You and everyone else," she said, then opened the door, so I could see all the flowers and covered pans with food in them. "Come on in."

I followed her inside. The house was dark and had a musty smell to it. We walked to her kitchen, and she put the chocolates down. There was hardly room on the counter for all the food.

"I don't know why everyone seems to think lasagna is

what you need when you lose your child," she said. "I can't fit it all in my fridge. Please, take one home with you."

"How are you?" I asked.

"How am I? Well…I guess…at least, I finally got closure, right? That's what they all tell me. But I didn't want closure. I wanted my daughter back. I want to hold her in my arms. I want to be down on that beach watching her surf. I want to drive her to North Carolina this weekend for the nationals."

I sighed. "It must be tough. I can't even imagine."

Jenna grabbed a photo of Sophie from the fridge and looked at it. "This was her first time surfing. She stood up on her first try. Look at her face. She was so happy. I never could get her out of the water ever since. She lived and breathed for that sport. It was her everything. I wanted her to have that dream come true. To be able to live off of what she loved."

"I can't blame you," I said. "It's great when they find something they're passionate about. You want to encourage them. I think all mothers would."

"Only now, I can't help thinking I made a mistake. I should never have pushed this life on her. It was too early. She could have waited. Maybe the killer wouldn't have targeted her. She was in the public eye, you know? It can be dangerous. Someone stalks her or thinks he's her father or something like that."

"Someone stalked her?" I asked.

Jenna nodded. "Last year. This guy started writing messages on her Facebook profile. She has it for sponsor reasons, but I'm the one who manages it. We found out he was at her contests and had been watching her for a long time. At one of them down in Melbourne Beach, he showed up with flowers that he gave her. The card said something nasty about him not being able to wait until she was his. We had the police on it. Gave him a restraining order."

"Has he been questioned?" I asked.

"I sure hope so. But they don't tell me anything. All I can

do is just sit here and wait for more bad news. I'm not sure I can take anymore, you know? I just want to see him be put away, so he won't hurt anyone else."

"Who was he, the stalker?" I asked.

"He lived in Rockledge, I think. The creepiest part was I had seen him at so many of the contests. He was always cheering Sophie on and taking pictures, but I just assumed he was one of the photographers. There are so many of them that hang out down there. I just never realized he was only taking pictures of my daughter. The police said he had his computer filled with them. They also told me it wasn't unusual with a child like her being in the spotlight the way she was. That was when I started getting nervous for her."

I nodded, then spotted a picture of Sophie with her dad holding a surfboard between them.

"What about her father?" I asked. "I understand there was trouble during the divorce?"

Jenna scoffed. "You can say that again. The bastard tried to take me for half of Sophie's money. But the money isn't mine. It's hers. I've put it away for her college education. That was actually part of why I divorced him. He was obsessed with her career and making money off of her. I kept telling him she was our daughter and she was allowed to have a childhood, but he believed she had to perfect her game constantly and he pushed her way too hard. He would come home in the middle of the day and take her surfing if there was the least bump on the ocean, even if she was having friends over or was in the middle of her schoolwork. She loved surfing, so it wouldn't make her mad, but he would stay out there for hours with her, yelling at her till she got one maneuver right. Sometimes she would be so exhausted she couldn't even eat when she came home, and she would wake up at night screaming, having nightmares about losing a final. She was so afraid of disappointing him that it was hurting her. He would always yell at her if she came in from a heat and he didn't think she had done well enough. I couldn't get him to stop and, finally, I threw him out. My parents bought the house for us, so I could stay here while he had to go live in some condo. He never forgave me. And then...well, as soon as I threw the D-word out there, I don't know what happened to him. I didn't recognize him anymore. It was like he became someone completely different. At one point, he even tried to turn Sophie against me, telling her I was crazy, and I was the one trying to push her, so I could make money off of her. It was all a mess."

I nodded again, remembering how Chad had changed overnight, how the man that I loved suddenly had turned into my worst enemy, and I had seen hatred in his eyes where there had once been love. A love that had brought us three wonderful children.

"You think he could hurt Sophie?" I asked. "I know it's hard to imagine about a man you once loved."

She threw out her hands, a tear escaping her eye. "I don't know, to be honest. I feel like I don't even know him anymore."

Chapter 18

SHE WAS late for the bus, again, and just as she ran out of the condominium and into the street, she spotted it passing her.

"Shoot!"

Maddie bit her lip, not knowing what to do now. That bus was her only means of transportation. She looked back up at the window to her condo, wondering if she should just stay home. But she had missed so much school lately that she risked being held back again. Nine days were all they could be absent in a semester if they didn't have a doctor's note. And she never did. Her mom couldn't afford to take her to the doctor.

Maybe I could walk to school?

Maddie looked down the street. It wasn't that far, was it? She would be late, yes, but at least she would be there. A tardy was hardly as bad as a day of absence. She looked down at her shoes, where her big toe was peeking out from a hole in the right one. She wondered if the shoes would last for that long of a walk. Her mom would get so angry with her if she had to buy her new shoes already. They cost a fortune, even though they were from a thrift store. And that was money she could have used on food and rent.

Maddie looked at her T-shirt. It had a big stain on the front, but it was the best she could do. There were no clean ones this morning, and this was the one that looked the best. The other kids were going to laugh at her and point it out, but she didn't care. She had to not care. It was the only way of surviving. Rosa, her pit-bull, was barking from the window, and that made her laugh. Rosa was her best friend and the one who protected her when her mom was working at night. She could sometimes be gone for days, but luckily, Maddie had Rosa to keep her company. They would eat cereal from the box or toast waffles in the toaster and eat them together. The neighbors were often fighting at night and yelling loudly, but then Rosa would jump into Maddie's bed and lie close to her, making her feel safe, and she would be able to fall asleep, even if they threw stuff out the windows, which sometimes happened. During the daytime, the neighbors were nice enough and sometimes the lady, Matilda, would give Maddie a cookie if she sat out on the stairs when Matilda came home from grocery shopping. But once darkness fell, the yelling started all over again. Maddie's mom had once told her it was because that's when they had too much to drink and then they would fight over something stupid. Maddie didn't understand why they just didn't drink all those beers. Then they wouldn't fight, and everyone would get better sleep.

But it wasn't as simple as that, her mom had explained, then added that she would understand once she was older.

Maddie wasn't sure she wanted to grow older if it meant drinking too much and staying up all night yelling at one another. Or if it meant she'd have to work all night like her mother, getting beaten up by strangers because she didn't do her job well enough.

No, Maddie was very happy being a child, she thought to herself as she began to walk down the street in the direction of her school. She had only taken a few steps out of the parking lot before a car stopped by her side and the window was rolled down.

"Hey there, little girl. Where are you going?"

Maddie couldn't really see the face of the person talking to her because of the strong sun coming from behind the car, but she was certain she knew the voice and moved closer.

"To school," she said.

"Are you walking all the way to school from here? You'll be late," the voice said.

Maddie shrugged. "I missed the bus."

"Again? Someone's gotta learn how to get up earlier in the morning. How about I take you there, huh?"

Maddie looked at the face, then hesitated. She stood for a few seconds, contemplating what to do. Then she remembered her teacher's face the last time she had been late. Maddie smiled widely, then ran to the passenger seat and opened the door, yelling, "That would be awesome. Thank you!"

Chapter 19

WHEN LEAVING JENNA'S HOUSE, I should have gone home and continued unpacking. It was my plan to, it really was, but while driving down Jenna's street, I couldn't stop thinking about the dad and what Jenna had told me. Ever since I had heard about Sophie's disappearance, I had been wondering about the father and why they didn't seem to consider him a suspect.

So instead of going home, I grabbed my phone and called my dad. If anyone knew where Sophie's dad lived, it was him. He knew everything around here, and I was right. A second later, I had an address, and I hung up after my dad had reminded me that *I was no longer working for the FBI* and that *it was time for me to rest and lick my wounds*.

I knew he was right, but still, I couldn't just leave this alone. I was curious and needed to know.

So, I went. After all, it was only a few blocks away and would hardly take long. I drove onto his street and parked. I knew these condos very well. When growing up, they had been the place our parents told us to avoid. It was the type of place where the rent was cheap, and the owners didn't do background checks, so anyone could live here, even if they had a record. Growing up, I had been taught to ride my bike on the other side of the street and to never talk to anyone here. All us kids were terrified of the people living there. There would always be these men standing outside on the grass, with big dogs that would growl at you when you passed them.

Now, as I came here as an adult, the place didn't seem so terrifying anymore. More tragic than anything. There was an old man sitting on a chair outside, his old dog lying beneath him. He barely looked up when I walked past him and inside the building.

I rang Todd Williams' doorbell, but there was no answer. After ringing the second time, I decided it was time to go. I had nothing much to do there anyway. This wasn't my case, and I had my plate full as it was. I turned around to walk away, when someone came up the stairs, a golden retriever walking up a few steps ahead of him. I recognized his face from the pictures I had seen in the papers and on Jenna's fridge.

His red eyes spotted me, and his lips started shivering. "Who are you? If you're a reporter, you'd better get the hell out of here."

I shook my head. "No. No. I'm not."

His eyes grew milder. "Oh, okay."

The puppy sniffed my legs, and I reached down to pet him. "He's gorgeous," I said. "How old?"

"Four years. He's a rescue."

I knelt next to the dog and petted him, then let him lick my cheek. "A rescue, huh? Golden retrievers aren't that common as rescues, are they?"

"No, I got lucky."

I giggled as the dog got playful. Todd walked to the door and opened it with his key.

"Say, haven't I seen your face somewhere before?" he asked. "I know where. You're that FBI lady."

I looked at him, startled. "You heard about me?"

"I read one of your books," he said. "I'm a geek when it comes to stuff like that. You know with serial killers and all that. I like the real stuff, not all the fake stuff on TV like CSI this and CSI that, but the real true crime. I read all of it."

"Really?"

"Yes, say, could I get you to sign my book? That would be so cool."

I nodded, thinking this was easier than I had expected. I didn't even have to lie.

"Sure. If you have a pen?"

Todd's face lit up. "Yes, yes, of course. Come on in."

Chapter 20
THEN

THE BOY STOOD by the window. As a car drove onto the street, he winced, thinking it had to be her. But as the car continued past his house, his heart sank again.

He felt a hand on his shoulder and looked up. It was his dad. He smiled at the boy.

"She'll be here, son. Soon."

The boy looked at his backpack on the floor. He had packed it the night before, knowing he was going to spend the next five days at his mom's place. His sister sat on the couch, playing with her dolls. She too had her coat on and her backpack packed, but other than that, she didn't seem to care much about what was going on. Didn't she know that Mommy was late?

"What if she forgot?" the boy asked. "Like last time?"

His dad shook his head. "She won't. Last time was just a misunderstanding, remember? She thought it was next weekend instead. Your mom gets busy, you know. Sometimes, she gets the days mixed up."

The boy nodded. His dad had explained to him that it was just a misunderstanding. It wouldn't happen again. Last time had been horrible. The boy had waited and waited all weekend, but his mother never came, and then the following weekend, his dad had taken him camping, and when they came back, they had found their mother sleeping in her car in the driveway. She had been angry and yelled at his dad for taking the boy away on her weekend, and they had ended up yelling at one another and the boy hadn't been able to spend time with his mom at all since, during all the yelling, his dad had told her to leave because she was crazy and too upset for him to trust her with the children. Then, right before he shut the door, he had called her high. The boy had meant to ask him what that meant, but he hadn't dared.

Another car drove up the street, and the boy turned to look, flocks of butterflies fluttering in his stomach. Maybe this time it would be her; it had to be, right? His dad had told him she would be there at eight o'clock in the morning, and last time he asked his dad for the time, he had said it was ten. The boy didn't know much math or about time in general, but he did know that ten was way past eight. And that meant she was late. Again.

The car drove close to the house, but it passed too. The boy sighed and looked up at his father, who smiled again.

"She'll come, son. Don't worry."

But he was worried. He was very worried that she wouldn't come. Not just for his sake, because he really missed his momma, but also for his little sister. She had cried several times this week because she missed her mom.

"Momma?" she said from the couch, looking up from what she was doing. The boy had told her all morning over breakfast how wonderful it was going to be to see their mom and spend five days with her again, but now he was regretting it.

The boy shook his head. "No Momma. Not yet."

His father sighed and sounded tired. He was worried too, the boy could tell, and grabbed his hand in his.

"Why doesn't Mommy want to be with us, Daddy?" he asked.

His dad let out a heartfelt sigh. "I don't know, son. I just don't think we're good enough for her anymore."

The boy nodded and glanced at his baby sister while biting his lip. Then he shook his head.

"We don't need her, Daddy."

His dad chuckled and ruffled his hair. "You're so right, son. We have each other, and that's all that counts."

Chapter 21

"WE CAME to Cocoa Beach when Sophie was just three years old," Todd said and looked at his daughter's picture. "That's when she tried surfing for the first time...on one of those big soft-top boards that you can rent by the beach. I pushed her into the wave, and she stood up. On the ground, she would stagger around and often fall, but on that thing, she was steady as a rock. She was a natural, and I saw it right away. I had grown up surfing myself, with Kelly and the boys back then, but never made it very far. I could just see that she had a gift, and I signed her up for surf camp that same summer. In the beginning, it was all just fun and games, but she developed her skills so fast we couldn't ignore it. By the time she was five, she surfed better than I did. Her learning curve was amazing."

I nodded and sipped the coffee Todd had served me. I had signed his book and slowly led the conversation onto his daughter and, luckily for me, he was more than willing to talk about her. It was something I had experienced lots of times in my line of work. People who had recently lost someone often needed to talk about them, talk about how amazing they had been.

"This is from her first contest," he said and showed me a picture on his phone. "I was the one to push her into the waves back then. And she won, of course."

I smiled. "You look very proud," I said and studied the picture of him holding the big trophy.

"Proudest moment of my life. Since the birth of Sophie, naturally." A shadow moved over his face as the memory faded and he returned to the harsh reality. "I thought she would make it on the World Tour one day; I really did. I thought she would be the next Kelly. I mean once she was ten and everyone talked about her, all the magazines and so on, they started saying it. Never had this town seen such a big talent since Kelly Slater. Of course, I wanted her to reach her full potential."

"You and your wife had a falling out, I understand?" I asked.

He chuckled. "That's very diplomatically put. She was the one who wanted the divorce, not me. Suddenly, she decided to throw me out and keep me away from Sophie. I never fully understood why. My best guess is she wanted to keep the money for herself. It was all Jenna's mother's doing if you ask me. She never liked me and kept telling Jenna to take the money and run. She thought Jenna did all the hard work because she homeschooled the girl. But I sacrificed myself too, you know. I was a chef, but once Sophie started to really get serious, and we traveled constantly, I couldn't keep it up. They sacked me, and here I am. No job and no daughter. Can you blame me for at least trying to get some of the money? I had worked hard to get Sophie to where she was. I was broke, and I only thought it was fair that I got my cut. Jenna just took everything, and I wasn't even allowed to see the girl. In court, she told the judge that I had molested the child. She even had some blood in Sophie's underwear to prove it, she said. It was so messed up. She would do anything to keep the girl to herself. And then look what happened."

"You say she believed she was molested?" I asked.

Todd sighed and rubbed his forehead. "Yeah, but you can't believe anything that woman says. She's such a liar. I don't even think she knows what's true and what isn't anymore. She told the judge all these lies about me and, of course, he ended up giving her full custody. I didn't even get to say goodbye, and now…she's…well, it's all her fault. If she hadn't told Sophie to go on that Girl Scout trip. What was she even doing there? You can't surf in the middle of the country. She was wasting her time. She should have been training for her next competition." Todd sighed and leaned back in his worn-out leather couch that he told me came with the fully furnished condo he had rented. "Ah, what does it matter anyway? It's all too late now. We'll never know what she could have amounted to."

I nodded, sipping my coffee, wondering about this news, when I realized it was getting late. I had to get back. I rose to my feet, thanked Todd for his time, then walked to the door, where I stopped.

"She had a coach, right?"

"Oh, yes. I couldn't get her to where she was on my own."

"Who was he?"

"Thomas Price. He's a local boy. Was on the World Tour for two years before he was injured. He could have been big too but never made it any further. It was his back. Too bad. It's a story you'll hear a lot around here. Lots of broken dreams walking around this town."

Chapter 22

I MADE it to Publix and, while I pushed my cart through the aisles, pulling down milk—getting two gallons this time—and eggs, I called Matt.

"This is a nice surprise."

I smiled. "I thought I'd check in on you. How are you holding up?"

"Eh."

"That well, huh?"

"This isn't exactly a trip to Disney."

"I spoke to the mother today. I went to check in on her," I said. "See if she was all right. Pay my respects."

"Are you doing police work?" he asked. "I thought you were done with all that?"

"I am. I just...well, I was curious, and then I wanted to make sure..."

"You do realize we've already talked to her? I'm a highly trained detective. I don't have much experience, but I know how to perform an investigation."

"Of course, you have. And, of course, you do. I didn't mean to...imply that...I just asked a little about Sophie and the divorce and all that."

Matt sighed. "I've been over that…"

"Did you know there was a stalker?" I asked, cutting him off.

"Of course," he said. "He was the first person we had in."

"And?"

"He had an alibi for the day she went missing. He was in south Florida visiting his aunt at a nursing home in Ft. Lauderdale. Lots of witnesses saw him at dinner."

"He could have driven back. She was taken late at night," I said.

"He spent the night there. In his aunt's room, sleeping on a sofa."

I nodded, grabbed a pack of sliced American cheese, and put it in the cart. "I'm not completely convinced, but okay. How about the claims that Sophie was molested?"

"Wow, you've been busy," Matt said. "Yes, we talked to her mother about that. She made the claims in court, but no charges were ever made. There was no investigation into the matter. She withdrew the claims while the custody case was still ongoing."

I stopped. "She withdrew it, why?"

Matt sighed. "I don't know, listen…"

"I know. You're tired. You sound awful, Matt. Have you slept at all? I know how cases like these can take a toll on…"

"Eva, stop, will you? I've got this. I can do it. The chief has given me the case and wants me to solve it. As much as I appreciate your involvement—and I do—I need to get back to work."

"Are you working on it alone?" I asked, startled.

"No. I have a partner, but the chief put me in charge."

"Who is your partner?"

"Nosy much, are we?" he said.

I grabbed a pack of freshly baked glazed donuts and put them in the cart, telling myself I'd diet next month.

"I...well, yes. I just thought I might know him, that's all. Is he from around here?"

"As a matter of fact, he is," Matt said. "And you do know him."

"I thought so," I grinned.

"It's Chris Cooper."

I stopped right in front of the candy aisle. "You're kidding me, right? Cooper who used to pick his nose in class? Who couldn't run ten feet without having an asthma attack?"

"The very same. But he's different now. Grew out of the asthma, I guess," Matt said. "Listen. I gotta go. Chief's calling my name."

"She's not. You're just trying to get out of this conversation," I said.

He chuckled. "Okay, yes, I am. I have tons of work to do."

"Before you go. What about the autopsy?" I asked.

"Should be in soon. I'm waiting for it."

"Okay. Well, good luck, and Matt?"

"Yes?"

"I'm rooting for you. Catch that bastard, so we can all sleep safely at night again, will you?"

He chuckled again. "I'm doing my best."

Chapter 23

I LOADED the car with all my groceries, then drove home and unpacked it all. I looked at the filled fridge and Jenna's lasagna on the counter with great satisfaction. I had bought all the kids' favorite things. I had forgotten how much I loved taking care of them and making them happy.

It hadn't been Chad who did all the work constantly. When they were younger, we had split it more evenly. He was at home and did most of it, but every now and then, I would come home early and cook or shop on my way home. I would even read stories for the children before bedtime and tuck them in. But as my workload grew and I traveled more, those precious moments stopped occurring, and Chad took over more and more. Suddenly, I no longer did any of those things, and I guess it was around then that we stopped talking as well. There was so much about my work I could never tell him, and since that was such a big part of my life, I just stopped telling him anything. On weekends, I would try and spend as much time as possible with the children, taking them to soccer or volleyball games, and slowly Chad started to resent me for always coming in from the sidelines and sweeping away the kids with my presence, only doing all the fun stuff. I guess I just thought being with the kids was more important and this was the only way I would get to. I neglected him and our marriage in the process. I guess I assumed he would still be there once the kids had grown up, that they were the ones I needed to cherish because, sooner or later, they would be gone. I had never imagined it would be the other way around.

The door swung open, and Olivia came in, still listening to music on her headphones. I smiled victoriously.

"Hi, hon. You hungry?"

She pulled out her headphones, then shook her head.

"No? I bought donuts. I thought we could make a cup of coffee and talk a little. How was your day?"

My daughter stared at me, eyes wide.

"I just ate. Literally. Me and Brooke just had an acai bowl at Café Surfnista."

"Oh. Really?"

"Yes, really."

"I thought you had volleyball practice this afternoon?" I asked.

"It was canceled. Coach had a thing."

"Oh, okay. So, no donut?"

She shook her head and walked to the stairs. "I have homework."

"Wait," I said.

She stopped at the foot of the stairs.

"Where's your sister? Don't you get out at the same time? If you went to Café Surfnista with a friend, then where is she?"

Olivia shrugged. "You don't know?"

"I know I'm probably supposed to, but no, I don't know. Enlighten me, please."

"She has choir. They're rehearsing for the concert."

"Ah, I see."

Olivia smiled. She was about to walk up to her room, then stopped herself at the foot of the stairs.

"It's okay, Mom. You know that, right?"

"What is?"

"That you can't keep track of our lives. It's normal. All the other moms are clueless too. Don't be too hard on yourself."

I swallowed and sent her a smile. "Okay. I'll remember that. Thanks."

"No problem."

Feeling good about myself for once, I sat down and sunk my teeth into a donut alone, when the door slammed open again, and Christine stormed inside. Her eyes gleamed with excitement. Seeing my daughter happy for once made my heart skip a beat.

"Is it fixed?"

I froze. "Is what fixed?"

"The computer. Did they fix it?"

My heart dropped, and my eyes fell on the laptop on the counter in the same spot where it had been since Saturday when she asked me to get it fixed.

Uh-oh.

Christine's eyes grew wide. "You didn't take it?"

I swallowed, then grabbed the computer under my arm. "You know what? I'll do it right now."

"Aren't you forgetting something?" Christine asked.

I looked at her, then remembered. "Alex! Shoot. It's Monday, and he is doing reading club and has to be picked up." I smiled, looking at my watch. I still had fifteen minutes before he was done.

"You know what? I'll just take him with me. I'll have that computer fixed in no time. Meanwhile, grab yourself a donut, do your homework, and then I'll be back in about an hour or two. Your sister is upstairs."

Christine smiled again. The sight made me relax.

"Thanks, Mom. You're the best."

I smiled and rushed out the door, feeling like I was finally getting the hang of this being a full-time mom thing. It wasn't about being perfect; they never expected that of me, but they did expect that I did the best I could.

Chapter 24

SHE WAS BEING PULLED by her hair and dragged across the floor. Maddie was screaming her heart out. Her scalp was hurting, and every bone in her body was aching from bumping against the stairs. She tasted blood in her mouth from the many punches she had received in the car. Her cheeks felt like they were on fire and her heart was thumping in her chest.

At first, she had cried and asked for it to stop, but the person wouldn't. The punches kept falling on her, and she had covered her face with her hands. Then they had stopped, and the car had started to move. Maddie had cried when they passed the road she knew led to the school and tried desperately to open the door, but it was locked. She had cried and kicked it, then received another punch, one so hard everything had gone black.

When she woke up again, the car had stopped in a strange place she didn't recognize. Then the door was pulled open, and she had been grabbed by the hair and dragged across the hard ground.

Now the pulling of her hair suddenly eased up, and she plopped down on a carpet, crying and spitting out blood.

"Please," she said. "I just wanna go home."

She looked up at the perpetrator, her eyes pleading for mercy. But as their eyes met, she knew there was no pity to receive. There was hardly even humanity. She had seen that look in the eyes of the men her mom sometimes brought home. The ones that left her mom with bruises, even though Maddie could hear her pleading with them not to since she wouldn't be able to work if she was beat up.

"I want my mommy," she said, nevertheless.

For years, Maddie had been alone with her mother. It had been just the two of them, getting by the best they could. She had a dad somewhere, but she could hardly remember him anymore. They used to be together, her parents. The first couple of years of her life, they lived in a house, her mother had told her—not a big one, but one good enough for the three of them. It was a real house with a small backyard. Maddie had always dreamt about living in a house with a backyard she could play in.

"Did we have a swing?" she had asked her mom.

"We could have had one," her answer sounded. "If we had stayed there."

"Why didn't we, Mommy?"

"Because your dad left. I couldn't afford to keep it alone. I didn't have a job. I never had an education. That's why I always tell you to get an education, okay? I worked where I could, but never managed to keep a job very long. Then I met Tommy. And now I'm making a lot more money than I ever did. Enough to take care of you and make sure you get a proper education, okay? So, you work hard now, you hear me? It's hard out there, baby. Life is tough. Always remember that."

Her perpetrator looked down at Maddie with those dark eyes, then tied her hands and her legs together using zip tie strips. He then put a blindfold over her eyes and pressed a dirty, bad-tasting cloth into her mouth. He almost choked her when taping her mouth over so she couldn't move her lips. The feel of the cloth inside of her mouth made her gag. She was left lying on her side with the carpet rubbing against her pounding cheek.

Maddie heard the footsteps of her perpetrator leave and then there was nothing but a deep scary silence.

Chapter 25

ALEX WAS in an excellent mood when I picked him up and, together, we drove the long way to Vieira and the Apple store. The guy behind the counter told me they would take a look at the computer, but they'd have to keep it overnight and then call me with their diagnosis. I texted Christine the news, to make sure she was prepared not to have her computer for yet another day, and she texted back that it was okay.

Then we left the store and drove back. I felt happy and sang along to Bruno Mars, my son screaming his little heart out in the back seat, singing along as well. He wasn't exactly musically talented, and his singing was way out of tune, but boy, he loved to sing. And he loved being allowed to use his voice. I knew he had to keep it down in school all day and that his teachers were constantly on his case to get him to be quiet, so I figured it did him good every now and then to be able just to scream and have no one yell at him.

We drove up A1A and passed the gas station when suddenly I noticed a bunch of police cars passing me and stopping in a driveway a little further down. I drove past slowly and spotted a massive amount of police officers in the same driveway.

"That was odd," I said and looked at Alex in the rearview mirror. He stared at them too, pointing his finger at them. No one loved blinking lights and sirens more than him.

Curious as to what was going on, I parked the car and told Alex to stay there for a few seconds. Then I hurried toward the house, where a few neighbors had already gathered in front of the big beach mansion.

"What's going on?" I asked a random man standing there.

He shook his head. "They say his son is missing. Never came home from school."

"Couldn't he just be with some friends?" I asked.

The man shrugged. "I guess."

"Who lives there?" I asked.

"Senator Pullman."

My eyes grew wide. "So, he's the son of a senator?"

The man nodded. I spotted Matt walking out of the house and rushed up to him. A police officer tried to stop me, but Matt told him I was okay. He could let me in.

"What's going on?" I asked. "Senator Pullman's son is missing?"

Matt wrinkled his forehead. "I…how do you know this already?"

"Does it matter?" I asked. "Do you think he might have been kidnapped?"

Matt exhaled. He nodded. "The senator was sent a video on Facebook."

"Are they asking for a ransom?" I asked.

"It's not like that."

"Then, what is it? What was on the video?"

"I really shouldn't be discussing these things with you," he said. "You handed in your badge. You're like a civilian now."

I lifted both eyebrows. "What was on the video, Matt?"

Matt sighed again. He never could say no to me—not when we were kids, and not now.

"It was a clip. Showing the son sitting in a chair, tied up, crying helplessly."

I stared at him. "And what else? A ransom request?"

He shook his head. "That's it. That was all it was."

"But you are tracing the video, right?"

"I've called for help from the county's IT department, but they're all the way in Rockledge."

"But until then, you need to find the boy before it's too late," I said pensively. "Can I take a look at the video?"

Matt sighed. "I don't know…why?"

"Can it harm anyone that I take a look?" I asked.

He shook his head. "Probably not. Come with me."

I paused. "I kind of have my son in the car. Let me go get him first…"

Matt stared at me, then chuckled. "Of course, you do."

Chapter 26

MATT SHOWED me into the huge mansion. I was holding Alex by the hand, nodding politely at every police officer I saw. Alex stared at them with wide-open eyes and muttered under his breath:

"Cool."

"This is FBI-profiler, Eva Rae Thomas. She's gonna help us find your son, Nathaniel."

Matt presented me to the senator. He was sitting in his massive kitchen with high vaulted ceilings, his wife next to him, her long fingernails tapping nervously on the side of an empty coffee cup.

I reached out my hand and shook the senator's. He looked at me, impressed.

"FBI? That was fast."

"I was in the area," I said.

Alex made a loud noise sounding like a siren, and the senator and his wife stared at him. I sent them both a smile, then looked at Matt.

"Over here," he said and guided me to a laptop.

Alex had his eye on a beautiful Goldendoodle who was

wagging his tail and holding a tennis ball in his mouth. Alex whined and started to pull away from me.

Matt was about to start the video when I stopped him. "Can you take Alex, please? Just for a sec?"

Matt looked confused. "Take him?"

"Just entertain him while I watch this. And no matter what you do, don't let him get his hands on that tennis ball in the dog's mouth. He'll throw it, and something will break. Believe me; you don't want that."

Matt held back a chuckle, then stretched out his hands toward Alex. "Hi there, buddy. Say, have you ever seen a real police baton?"

My eyes grew wide. "Don't. He'll break stuff."

Matt smiled. "I'm not going to let him hold it, just show it to him. Now, go watch that clip, and I'll handle him, okay? Don't worry."

I cleared my throat, then walked back to the computer, still keeping one eye on my son. He and Matt were talking for a little while and then Matt took him by the hand, and they started to walk outside to the pool area. I stared in their direction, wondering how long it would take before Alex would begin to yell something or scream, but it didn't happen. The two of them seemed to be deeply engaged in their conversation, and Alex looked up at him with big admiring eyes.

"Well, I'll be…" I mumbled under my breath, then pressed the play button on the computer.

The clip wasn't more than twenty seconds and showed the senator's son sitting in a chair, hands and feet tied to it. The boy was crying. He had to be about fifteen or so, judging from the light hairs growing on his upper lip. The clip was nothing but just him sitting there, and then it was over. I played it again, then again, and once more until I finally stopped it midway.

"You seeing something?"

The voice was familiar, yet so different that I wasn't sure. I turned around and looked into the eyes of Chris Cooper; only this was nothing like the Cooper I had known in high school. Only the eyes gave him away. The rest, well…the rest was quite a different story. He was tall, but he had always been one of the tallest boys in school. What he didn't have back then were those broad shoulders and buff arms. I didn't quite recall that jawline either or those abs.

"Cooper?"

"They told me you were back," Cooper said, then gave me a hug. "I can't believe it. How have you been?"

I grimaced. "Eh."

"Yeah, I heard about your divorce. What an idiot, huh? Leaving a woman like you?"

I blushed just as Matt came back into the room, still holding Alex's hand. He looked at the two of us with an odd expression.

"Anything?" he asked, sounding almost mad.

I nodded and took Alex in my arms. "As a matter of fact, yes."

I turned and showed them both the computer, then pointed. "Look at that. There's a window behind him. Even though the blinds are pulled, you can still see the shape of it, if you look closely. There's only one place in this town that has windows that are diamond-shaped like that."

Both men's eyes grew wide. "She's right," Matt said. "I can't believe I didn't see it. Thank you."

I shrugged. "To be honest, it was almost too easy."

Chapter 27

I FOLLOWED the police cars in my minivan, and we parked in front of the townhouses. I made sure to park on the other side of the street, to keep away if something went bad. It was a row of about six small houses that had been built in a certain style back in the seventies. They were known to be cheap to rent but located right across the street from the beach. Most people thought it was a shame that such ugly houses were situated in such a lucrative spot. Others thought they were worth preserving because of their unique architectural style, with their diamond-shaped windows and draped roofs.

"So, which one do you think it is?" Matt asked as I got out of the car. I left the engine on, and Alex stayed in the car.

I looked up at the sun. "The video. It said in the corner that it was recorded at eleven o'clock...earlier today. There was sunlight coming in through the window behind him, which tells me he was sitting in one of those facing the street," I said and pointed.

"So, one of those two?" he asked.

I nodded. He gave me an unsure smile and put a hand on his weapon. "You better stay here."

I smiled and glanced back at Alex in the car. I had left the music on, blasting out of the speakers, and told him to sing as loud as he could, just in case. I didn't want him to hear anything.

Matt and his colleagues walked to the two front town-houses and knocked on both doors.

"Police. Open up!"

A small wave of excitement rushed through my body and, for just a second, I missed being back in the field. I just hoped they would find the boy alive.

One door was opened, and an elderly woman peeked out. "What's going on here?"

"We need to check your house, ma'am," Cooper said.

The old woman looked afraid. "W-why?"

Meanwhile, no one opened the door to the house next to it, and Matt pulled the handle. The old woman next door saw it.

"No one lives there anymore," she said. "It's been vacant for the past year."

Matt sent me a look, then mouthed, *should I?* I nodded in agreement. Matt knocked his shoulder into the door, and it opened easily. Then he disappeared inside, holding his gun tightly in his hand. I felt my heart rate go up and looked back at Alex, who had no idea what was going on. He was singing his heart out and swinging his toy ax around.

Not a sound came from inside the townhouse, and I felt scared for Matt for a short second. He came back out looking sick to his stomach.

"Matt?"

He closed his eyes for a brief moment. His eyes were brim-ming with horror. I rushed to him.

"Matt? Are you okay? What happened?"

Cooper stopped talking to the old lady and ran to him.

"I...I found him," he said.

"Who?" Cooper asked. "The senator's son?"

I could hear Matt's ragged breathing. He was fighting his tears. His answer came as a silent nod.

Chapter 28

I HAD PREPARED myself for something bad, but what I saw still pulled all the air out of me, like a punch to my stomach.

I walked inside first, Cooper coming up right behind me. The townhouse was completely empty. No furniture, only an old refrigerator was humming in the corner of the kitchen.

We found the senator's son in the living room in front of the fireplace, the diamond-shaped window behind him just like we had seen in the video. He was still tied to a chair, but unlike in the video, he was no longer fighting or crying. He was sitting completely still with his head slumped to the side. His eyes were still open, staring eerily at us like they were asking us why we were so late, why we were too late.

In his mouth, someone had stuffed hundred-dollar bills. A handful of them had fallen to his lap and the wooden floors beneath him.

"My God," Cooper said and clasped his mouth. He turned away like he couldn't bear to look at it.

I exhaled, fighting to keep calm. The boy was only a few years older than my Olivia. Probably even went to the same school, like all the kids in this town. This was unbearable.

"I called it in," Matt said, returning. His color had come

back, but he still looked sick. "Who does this? What kind of a sick pervert kidnaps a kid and kills him, stuffing money down his throat like that?"

I stared at the boy, then shook my head, realizing this wasn't my case and I had a son in my car. Suddenly, I just wanted to get back to be with my children.

"I'll guess I have to go notify the parents," Matt said.

"I should go," I said. "I'm not supposed to be here, and you guys have work to do."

"It was nice to see you again, Eva Rae," Cooper said and gave me a warm hug, holding onto me for a few seconds too long.

"Maybe I'll see you around?"

"We'll have to see about that," I said, and I turned around and walked away. Matt stared at me, then walked out in front of me. His steps were suddenly big and angry. He scoffed loudly.

"What?" I asked, baffled.

He shook his head. "Nothing."

I stopped. "What's going on here? Matt?"

He stopped too, then gave me a look.

"You don't think it's a little early? Not to mention inappropriate, given the circumstances?"

I couldn't believe my ears. "Excuse me?"

"Your divorce isn't even finalized yet, is it?" he asked as we came outside in the sunlight. I could hear the loud music blasting from inside my car. Alex was still at it. I could see his ax swinging through the air. That kid never ran out of energy. Chad used to say he was like that Energizer Bunny. I thought he was exaggerating back then, but now I understood what he meant.

"You thought I was flirting? I can't believe you," I said and grabbed the door handle.

"What?" he asked.

"Jealous much, are we?"

He gave me a look, then shook his head. "Don't flatter yourself. You've gotten really snooty, do you know that? You come here, big and mighty, and think you can tell us how to do everything. Well, we were doing just fine till you got here."

"Wow," I said and opened the door. "I guess I won't flatter myself and think you actually want me here. If you don't want me to help you out on this case, I don't have to. I'll walk away right now."

"Yeah…I think we've got it from here."

"All right," I said and got in. "Good to know."

Chapter 29

I COULDN'T BELIEVE HIM. I drove home, fuming. I felt so angry that I started unpacking right away and, by dinnertime, I had gone through two more boxes. My mom had called and invited us over for dinner, so I put the lasagna back in the fridge, got ready, and walked over there with the kids since they only lived two blocks down. My mom opened the door.

"I guess late is better than never, right?" she said, then looked at me. "What's happened to your hair? Did you do something to it?"

I felt it, then shook my head. "I stopped washing it. I'm going to try for dreadlocks. I think I might look good with them, don't you? Kind of get that Bob Marley thing going that I've wanted for years."

My mom stared at me, eyes wide. Then, realizing I was kidding, she gave me one of her annoyed smiles.

"Get in."

We walked into the living room. My parents lived in a beautiful house on the canal. It was huge, way too big for two people to live in alone, but they loved it there. It was my childhood home, but going there didn't exactly bring back fond memories. I had always hated living in a house where I had to be careful where I sat because the furniture was so expensive. I often joked that the furniture was more important to my mother than me. Except it wasn't a joke. It was often the truth. It got more of her attention than I ever did.

Christine went to sit on a couch, and my mom saw her, then rushed to grab a towel and placed it where she was going to sit.

"There you go," she said. "Jeans can leave a mark."

Christine gave me a look for help, and I nodded to tell her to simply indulge her grandmother. Olivia sat next to her, making sure to sit close enough so she was on the towel as well. I wasn't so worried about the girls as much as I was Alex. He had already finished two rounds of the living room, running with his toy ambulance, making loud noises. I gasped every time he passed the big human-sized sculptured vase that I knew my mom had shipped from Vietnam.

"Squirt!"

My dad came in, gave me a kiss on the cheek, then greeted the girls before catching Alex as he ran past him. He grabbed him around the waist and lifted him into the air, then spun him around till they both laughed.

"Jon!"

My mom came out of the kitchen, holding a tray with some sort of food on it.

My dad put Alex down. "Sorry, darling."

My mom gave him another look, then clapped her hands. "Appetizers, everyone. I made zucchini chips. Let's take them outside, shall we, so we can avoid greasy fingers on the furniture."

I exhaled, relieved. Outside, Alex could roam wild without breaking anything. Relieved, I sat down on the patio furniture while Alex took to the lawn and started somersaulting across the grass.

"So…" my dad said and sat next to me. He never got to say more before my mom came over too, interrupting us.

"Did you hear what happened to that senator's son? It was all over the news," she said, speaking with a low voice so the kids wouldn't hear. Olivia and Christine put on their swimsuits and went in the pool. I couldn't blame them. I wished I had done the same. It was too hot to just sit there.

"Of course, she did," my dad said. "She was there. I was just about to ask."

I turned to face him. "How did you know I was there?"

My dad smiled. "I know everything, remember? I see everything around here."

"Ah, don't listen to him, Eva Rae," my mom said. "Crystal called earlier and told us. I wasn't home, so he picked up."

Crystal was Matt's mother. Of course, Matt had told her I was there. I was beginning to remember why I was in such a rush to get out of this place twenty years ago. It was suffocating how everyone always knew everything you did.

"So, what do you think?" my dad asked.

"About the senator's son?" I shrugged. "I don't know, to be honest. It's all very strange. There was a video leading us to him. It was like the killer wanted us to find him. Like he had put the boy out on display. There was no ransom, no demands of any kind."

"It's horrifying," my mom said. "You hardly dare to go out anymore. Nowhere is safe."

"Do you think it was political?" my dad asked.

"That's what they said on TV," my mom added. "That he was targeted because of his father's job. Something about a bill he recently signed or maybe his stance on gun control. I don't know. It was all a little out there if you ask me."

"Yes and no," I said.

"What kind of an answer is that?" my mom said.

I bit my lip while watching Alex rolling on the grass. "I don't know yet. But I do think that choosing a senator's son has to have some sort of significance. I'm just not sure it's political. I think he might have chosen the senator's son because it would wake the interest of the media."

"You think the cases are connected, don't you?" my dad asked. "The surfer girl and the senator's son?"

I shrugged. "It's not really up to me to conclude anything. I stopped, remember? I am actually trying to stay away from this."

My dad nodded pensively. "You should be taking care of yourself and your children right now. Let someone else deal with this. Besides, you have that book to write. How's that coming along?"

I smiled, feeling guilty. "Eh. Not so much right now."

"Don't blow this one, Eva Rae," my mother said. "They might get angry with you at that publishing house and then where does that leave you? You have no additional income. You're a single mom now; your husband left you...you can't blow this too."

I glanced at my mom, then forced a smile. "Geez. Thanks for reminding me, Mom. I had completely forgotten how awful my life was."

My mom grimaced, then stood to her feet. "Oh, my, the food."

My mother rushed off, clacking along on her high heels. My dad leaned over and spoke with a low voice.

"She made curried quinoa with garbanzos and peppers. It's vegan, plant-based, and gluten-free. Does anyone even know what gluten is and why we're all suddenly allergic to it?"

I chuckled, then placed my arm around my dad's shoulder. "She means well. She wants you to stay healthy and stay with us for many years."

"I'm sixty-two. I'm not dying. Heck, I'm not even retired yet. I don't plan on going anywhere anytime soon. But I might if I don't soon get a big fat juicy steak."

I chuckled. You can always come eat from our fridge, Dad. Anytime you want a real meal, you just come over."

"It's good to have a backup plan," he said, whispering, while my mom yelled from inside the house that dinner was served.

After picking at my mom's food, pretending to eat, the kids and I went back home and played a card game, while eating Jenna's lasagna. We stayed up till ten o'clock, completely forgetting it was a school night. I wanted it to last forever. I couldn't stop thinking about those poor parents, the senator and his wife, who now sat alone in their big beach house without their child.

Chapter 30

THE FACELESS MAN is pulling my arm. It hurts, and I scream, but he grabs me around the mouth and tells me to shut up. His fingers taste like cigarettes. I am scared. I can hear my heart pounding. I can see my mom walking, pushing her cart, but she's too far away. I want to scream again, but I can't. I want to alert her to what is happening, but she's busy taking things from shelves; she doesn't notice; she doesn't even look in my direction.

"What are you doing?"

The voice coming from behind the faceless man is Sydney's. She's holding a doll in each hand and is staring at us. The man turns to look at her, then pauses.

I want to scream at her to get away, to go get Mommy, but I can't. Instead, I bite down on the man's finger so hard, he yelps and lets go of me. Heart pounding in my chest, I push myself out of his grip.

I opened my eyes, still feeling my heart pound in my chest. My mouth was dry, and I looked at the clock, then realized I had overslept.

I sprang to my feet, then ran into Alex's room. He was

already awake and sitting on the floor playing with his trucks, letting them crash into one another, making noises with his mouth.

"Alex. We're late. Get dressed."

He didn't react, but I felt certain he had heard me, so I moved on to the girls and woke them up one after the other. Olivia cursed and hurried to get dressed. Christine got sad and began to cry.

"I can't keep going in late, Mom. I'm gonna get in trouble for this."

"I'll write a note," I said. "Just get dressed and come down for breakfast. I'll drive you to school."

Christine sighed. "I hate this place. I miss Dad."

I paused and was about to say something, but then decided not to. It wasn't fair of me to demand that they never think about their father anymore. Fact was, he had abandoned us all, but the blow was especially hard on them since, for the past couple of years, he had been their entire world. He had been the only adult who took care of them. And just like that, he was gone. I cursed him inside my head, thinking I had no idea how to tell the kids that he didn't want them anymore, that now he wanted a new family. It was going to break their hearts. I wondered if I should have a talk with them about it, or simply let them find out on their own. Would they think I was just making it up if I told them? Because I was angry with him?

Probably. They adored their father, and in their eyes, he could do no wrong.

"I do too," I said. "But he's not here, and we have to try and do this on our own, honey."

"I don't want to," she said, crying. "I want him to come home."

I hugged her, not knowing what else to do. She cried for a few seconds, then stopped and wiped her eyes.

"Listen, honey. I know there are a lot of changes right now.

But I promise it'll get better, okay? You have to trust me on this."

She didn't say anything but got out of bed and put on her clothes. My heart was still bleeding as I served them cereal, for once having enough milk for them all and for my coffee. But right now, I wasn't sure milk was enough. They needed their father, and I loathed him for what he was doing to them.

Chapter 31

AFTER DROPPING THE KIDS OFF, I drove to the beach, my Yeti containing my coffee still in my hand. I had so much on my mind; I couldn't really face my house and the loneliness inside of it when the kids weren't there.

I felt exhausted. I hadn't slept well in a long time. The kidnapping of two kids since I got back here brought back too many bad memories.

I went for a walk and greeted a nice old couple who were obviously snowbirds. You could always tell by their pale skin and by how much they enjoyed the sunlight hitting their faces.

As I reached the pier, I stopped and watched the surfers. There were a couple of them out there. The waves were big and very glassy. One of the surfers stood out in particular as he shredded the waves and even went for some air. After watching him for a few minutes, he came up, and I realized it was Coach Price.

"Nice air," I said as he exited the water.

He smiled widely. "Thanks."

I sipped my coffee.

"Could you teach my kids to surf that well?"

He shrugged. "I don't really do beginners."

I nodded. "Of course not."

"But there's a really good surf school downtown. You can sign them up for camp and then maybe if they make it big, you can sign me on as coach. I can take them all the way."

"I'll remember that if we ever get that far," I said, chuckling at the idea of my kids surfing. It was mostly Alex I was thinking about. He needed a sport that could take some of the energy out of him. I looked at the coach, who was standing next to me, watching the other surfers out there.

"It doesn't hurt your back, surfing like that?" I asked.

"My back?"

"Yeah, you injured your back, didn't you? That's why you stopped on the tour?"

He nodded. "Ah, yes. No, I can do some stuff, just not all of what I used to be able to, and some days are better than others. Anyway. I should get back. Nice to meet you."

I looked after him, then smiled. "You too."

I stayed in my spot for a few minutes longer, sipping my coffee and watching the surfers, thinking about Sophie and Nathaniel, the senator's son, wondering why the killer—if it was the same one—had chosen those two kids of all the children he could have chosen. They were both very much in the spotlight and killing them had to have some significance. If it was the same guy, he clearly had some sort of message he was trying to get out. These kills weren't random.

I shook my head, once again reminding myself this wasn't my case, then began to walk back, planning my day in my mind. I would unpack a few more boxes and then sit down at my laptop and get some writing done. I needed to get at least the first page on paper today. I had written three books before this one and knew that the first page was mentally very important. Once you got that down, you had actually begun writing it, and then it would start to flow and come naturally. I just had to get past that first darn page. And for some reason, I kept postponing it.

Chapter 32
THEN

THREE YEARS LATER, the boy got a new mommy. She was beautiful, and the boy really liked her. He could tell his dad did too, and that made him even happier. She was very nice, even to his baby sister, and that made the boy happy. Having her at the house brought new joy, and it was like everything changed, especially his father, who no longer sat for hours in the living room, staring into thin air, saying nothing.

They told them to call her, *Mommy*. The boy found it a little strange at first since he already had a mommy. But his new mommy and his daddy had a new name for his old mommy. They called her The Thing. Every time they mentioned her, they would always say *The Thing said this* or *The Thing did that*. They also talked about her being on drugs and how it wasn't very good for the boy and his sister to visit her.

They didn't see each other often anymore. A couple of times a year. She kept getting the dates mixed up or missed the appointments, his dad and new mommy explained to him. It wasn't his fault, they kept saying, but it was hard for the boy not to feel a little guilty, to feel a little like his mommy didn't really want him.

"It's okay to be mad at her," his new mommy said one day when tucking him in. "She has not been treating you very well."

"The kids would sometimes come home with bruises," his dad said, coming in to say goodnight as well. "She hurt them when she was alone with them. And still, I can't say they can never see her again. I can't protect them. She's their mother."

"It's tough," the new mommy said.

And then they kissed.

Later that same night, the phone rang, and the boy hadn't fallen asleep yet, so he could hear his dad pick it up. He could tell it was his mommy or The Thing by the way his dad talked to her. He talked like he did when he was very angry with the boy or his baby sister. Like when they had gone to Michael's house down the street one afternoon without telling him. He talked to The Thing in the exact same way. Like he was mad.

The boy walked out of his room, and his dad saw him just as he hung up.

"What are you doing up, buddy?" he asked. "I thought you were asleep. You should be. It's a school night."

"Who was that on the phone?" he asked.

"That? Oh, it was no one. Wrong number. That's all. Don't you worry about that; just go to sleep."

"Was it Mommy?" he asked, rubbing his eyes.

"No. No, it wasn't. Now, go back to sleep."

The boy looked up at his father, then wrinkled his forehead. He had been so sure it was her, and he wanted to talk to her. He wanted to tell her he got a new bike. It had been so long since she had last called.

"It was no one. Now, get back to bed, buddy. You have school tomorrow."

"But…?"

"Now, I said. Now."

"Can I call her?"

"Can you call who?"

"Mommy. I want to call her."

His father scoffed. "Your mother doesn't want to talk to you. Don't you understand that? She abandoned all of us, and she doesn't want to see you. Now, get back to bed. I don't want to have to say it again."

The boy felt like crying. Still, he didn't. He held the tears back, then ran to his bed, cursing his mother far away, deciding he never wanted to see her again. Never.

Chapter 33

I FOUND ALL the baby pictures of Olivia, and that's when I stalled. Up until then, I had been through several boxes, and the kitchen was beginning to look decent. My mom would be pleased to see that all the plates were finally in place. She would probably find them to be ugly, yes, but at least they were there.

I told myself it was time for a cup of coffee and went through the baby books. I looked through them, lingering especially long on the ones from our trip to California when she was just a year and a half. I remembered the trip as exhausting because I spent most of the time running after her, but as I looked at the pictures, I was suddenly reminded of how simple life had been back then. I was nothing but a young detective with tons of dreams and aspirations of climbing the ranks one day. It had always been my ambition to get to the FBI, but back then, it had been nothing but an idea, a dream that I loved clinging onto.

I placed a finger on Chad's handsome face.

Gosh, I was in love with him back then.

My trip down memory lane was violently interrupted when there was a knock on my front door. It sounded urgent, and I hurried to open it. Outside stood Melissa. The look on her face told me something was very wrong.

"I need your help with something."

"Well, hello to you too. What's going on?" I asked. That was when I realized Melissa hadn't come alone. Behind her stood a woman that I had never seen before.

"This is Patricia," Melissa said. "She's actually the one who needs your help. Can we come in?"

"Sure. Sure," I said and stepped aside to let them in. "The place is still a mess, but what can you do, right?"

Patricia smiled at me feebly as she walked past me, and I closed the door behind them. I guided them into the kitchen and served them coffee.

"I think I still have some of that pie left," I said. "You want some?"

Melissa nodded. "Sure."

I found the plates and served us all some pie. Patricia barely touched hers.

"So, what's going on?" I asked midway through my piece. Unpacking had made me hungry, and I realized I had skipped lunch.

Melissa looked at Patricia, then at me. "Patricia has a request for you."

"Yeah?"

Melissa put her fork down. "Her daughter has gone missing."

I almost choked on my coffee. "Missing? What do you mean missing?" I looked at the woman next to me, then at Melissa for answers.

"She never came home from school yesterday," Patricia said.

My eyes grew wide. "Yesterday? But that's almost twenty-four hours ago?"

She nodded, heavily. "Yes, that's why I'm worried."

I couldn't believe what I was hearing. Knowing how

important the first twenty-four hours were when a child went missing, I couldn't believe they were just sitting there.

"But...but surely you filed a missing person's report? Have they had search teams out...to search the canals and the streets?"

Melissa stopped me. "That's the thing. She hasn't told the police."

"You haven't? But...why not?"

"She can't," Melissa said.

"And why is that?"

Patricia sighed. "I'm a prostitute. I work at night and leave my ten-year-old daughter home alone all night. I'm not happy about it, but it's the only way I can survive. I can't afford a babysitter, and I have no family nearby."

"If the police get involved, they'll take her daughter away," Melissa took over. "She can't go to the police; you must understand this, Eva. I told her it would be safe to come to you. We were hoping you could help find Maddie...without the police."

Chapter 34

IT WENT against everything I believed in. Everything I had been trained for and knew as the way to handle things, yet I still agreed to help her. How could I say no? Her daughter was missing.

I told them to take me to her condo, so I could look around. Patricia showed me in, grabbing the big pit-bull who ran for us as the door opened.

"This is Rosa. She won't harm you. She looks fierce but is like a lamb. She keeps Maddie safe at night."

I smiled and petted the dog.

"This is where she sleeps," Patricia said and opened a door.

It was the only bedroom in the condo. The mother slept on the couch.

"I never bring clients home anymore," she said, looking shameful. "I used to when she was younger, but then I realized how bad it was for her because she could hear it when they treated me badly. I was afraid she would begin asking questions. Now I have them take me to motels, or we just handle it in the car. So, I figured I might as well give her my bedroom."

I looked at the small woman in front of me, then felt like hugging her, yet slapping her at the same time. No one should have to live a life like this. Not the child who had no choice, not the mother who suffered abuse every day.

Patricia saw it on my face. She looked shameful.

"I tried getting other jobs, but…when I lost the one I had… well, I have to eat, right? I have my girl to feed. My ex refuses to pay anything."

"No one is judging you," Melissa said and placed a hand on Patricia's shoulder.

I smiled at her to reassure her that I wasn't, even though I had to admit that I had been at first. I was just suddenly so extremely grateful that I had made my own money and could take care of myself. Chad had promised he would pay alimony, but so far, I hadn't received any. He was still having the time of his life in Greece and not thinking about the kids or me. He had inherited a good amount of money when his mom passed recently, and I suspected that he was out burning all that off on his screaming midlife crisis. Luckily, the publishing house had given me a big advance, and I still had royalties coming from my previous books. If I didn't overspend, I'd be fine. And if everything went south, I always had my parents. My mother was cold and emotionally distant, yes, but I knew she and my dad would always bail me out if they needed to. I was one of the fortunate ones; Patricia wasn't.

"So, you say she left for school on Monday morning?" I asked and looked around the girl's room. Patricia had handed me a school photo of her daughter, so I knew what she looked like.

Patricia nodded. "Yes. I spoke to Mrs. Altman downstairs. From her window, she saw her walk to the road wearing her backpack, but she was too late. The bus had already been there. Mrs. Altman saw it pick up another kid from this block. But Maddie came out afterward. Before Mrs. Altman could come out on the porch to tell Maddie that she was too late, a car drove up on her side, and Maddie got in."

The blood in my veins froze. "She got into a car?"

Patricia nodded with a loud sob. "I just learned it this morning when I came down. I thought she was at a friend's house all day yesterday and I went to work in the evening, thinking she would be home later. I was preparing to scold her for being out so late. Then, when I came home this morning and could tell that Maddie hadn't been home all night, I panicked. I ran downstairs and knocked on Mrs. Altman's door to ask her if she had seen her and she told me this."

"I need to talk to this Mrs. Altman," I said. "Now."

Chapter 35

BEFORE WE LEFT Patricia's condo, I texted Olivia and asked her if she could be sure to be home when Alex came home with the bus today since I was out. He was usually about half an hour later than her if she came home directly from school and didn't go into town with her friends. Luckily for me, she texted me back that she had tons of homework, so she was planning on going home straight after school anyway. I was pleased with this. I needed my kids home today.

"Mrs. Altman?" I said as the old lady opened the door, leaning on her walker. A smile appeared on her weathered face.

"Yes?"

"My name is Eva Rae Thomas," I said. "I'm with the police. We're trying to figure out what happened to Patricia's daughter, Madeleine Jones. She told me you saw her get into a car?"

The old woman nodded. "Yes. It's true."

"What can you tell us about the car? Do you remember what it looked like? Maybe the color or the brand? Was there anything particular that stood out about it, like a sticker or anything?"

The old woman became pensive, and her face lit up. "I don't know any of those things since my eyes aren't what they used to be, but I did take a picture of it with my phone. I had a feeling that car was up to no good, and watching little Maddie get into it scared me. I knew something wasn't right. Wait here a sec while I go get my phone."

"You took a picture with your phone?" I asked, surprised.

The old lady returned a few minutes later, holding a phone in her hand. She pressed the screen and navigated through it like it was the easiest thing in the world.

"I love this thing. My daughter bought it for me, and I can't seem to stop using it. This is how I keep track of my grandchildren up north when she posts pictures on Facebook. The kids use Snapchat more, and we have over one hundred streaks. I send them pictures of myself wearing all these different filters; it's loads of fun. Keeps their old grandma on her toes. Here it is," she said. "It's not a very good picture since I took it as the car took off, but you can see some of it. Have a look for yourself."

I took the phone and looked. The car was definitely in motion when the picture was taken, making it a little blurry, but I could see that it was white, and I could see the shape of the driver. Unfortunately, I couldn't see a face, no matter how much I zoomed it in.

"There's more if you swipe sideways," she said.

I did, and to my excitement, there was a perfect picture of the license plate. This was our lucky day.

"Can you send me these two pictures, please?" I asked.

"I can airdrop them to you," Mrs. Altman said, as she touched the screen a couple of times, and then I had the pictures.

"Thank you so much, Mrs. Altman," I said and shook her hand. "You've been a tremendous help."

"You're very welcome. I just hope you find the girl. So

much bad stuff is happening these days. Find her and bring her back home, will you?"

"I will do my best, Mrs. Altman. I will do my best."

Chapter 36

I CALLED the station and asked to speak to Cooper. Patricia was sitting on her daughter's bed, biting her nails, while Melissa sat next to her and tried to calm her down. While waiting for Cooper to pick up, I saw Melissa pull out a pack of Kleenex from her purse and hand them to Patricia. The sight made me chuckle since I suddenly remembered how Melissa always took care of all of us back in the day. She always had a shoulder to cry on when you needed it and always had a piece of chocolate in her bag or a pack of Kleenex. It was just who she was. Always taking care of anyone in need.

"Miss me already?" Cooper said as he picked up.

"Very funny. No, I need your help."

"And Matt isn't your go-to guy anymore?" he asked. "That's new. Can't say I'm not flattered..."

I exhaled. What was this? Sixth grade?

"Matt and I aren't exactly...you know what? It doesn't really matter. That's not why I'm calling. This is urgent. I need your help. And I need you to be discreet about it."

"Sure. I guess I can do that," he said, sounding a little hesitant. I knew it was a lot to ask him.

"I need you to run a plate for me," I said.

He breathed, relieved. I don't know what he had feared I would ask him to do, but clearly, he had thought it was something bad. "I can certainly do that. Hit me."

I read the numbers for him, then waited while he put it in the system. I smiled confidently at Patricia to make her feel calmer. I hated seeing that look of despair in her eyes. I didn't even know how I would react if I didn't know where my child was and if I knew she had gotten into a car with some stranger. It would tear me apart with anxiety. It was unbearable to even think about, especially when thinking about what had happened to Sophie Williams and Nathaniel Pullman.

Cooper returned a few minutes later.

"I got it. It belongs to Thomas Price."

My eyes instantly grew wide. "Thomas Price?"

"Yeah, " he said. "Why are you checking up on him?"

I swallowed, thinking about Sophie and her mother.

"I have to go, Cooper. Thanks for helping me. I owe you one."

"But...?"

I hung up before he could ask any more questions. I stared at the name I had written on a piece of paper on Maddie's desk. I had seen this guy this same morning. Had he taken Maddie? If so, what had he done to her? Was she still alive or had he killed her? Was he also responsible for the death of Sophie Williams?

I wondered for a few seconds how to handle this. I knew Patricia was terrified of involving the police. She was absolutely right. If the police found out she had left her daughter alone all night, they would have to involve the DCF, and she would lose her child. I couldn't do that to her. But if this guy had taken Maddie, there was no time to waste. Not if we wanted to find her alive.

Chapter 37

MADDIE COULDN'T CRY ANYMORE. She had been crying so much her blindfold had gotten soaked, but now there were no more tears left in her. Her arms were strapped around her back so tightly they began to hurt, and she tried to sit up straight, but it was impossible when she couldn't use her hands to help. She tried anyway, using her elbow, but just as she managed to get herself almost up, she fell over and landed flat on her face.

Maddie cried out in pain as her cheek hit the carpet. She sobbed, feeling sorry for herself and so, so very hungry. Her prison guard had been there and poured water down her throat before pushing the bad-tasting cloth back into her mouth, so she felt like she was choking, taping it shut with duct tape. But she had welcomed the refreshing water in her mouth and throat. Now, she was mostly hungry, but so far, she had gotten no food at all while being held like this and she felt like she was about to die. Her stomach hurt so bad.

Maddie had felt this starving feeling before when they had run out of food, and her mother hadn't come home. Sometimes, she would be gone for days, working, she said, then come home with purple bruises all over her body. Maddie hated going hungry for days or waking up to an empty fridge. It was the worst. Actually, if she was honest, that wasn't the worst part about her life. The very worst part was the fact that all her friends knew what her mother did for a living. And they would tease her about it. Just the thought of how the kids in her class looked at her filled her with such deep shame it almost made her cry again.

One time, a boy from her class, Gareth, had held her down and spat in her mouth, telling her to get used to that feeling since she would grow up to be a whore too. That was the most humiliating thing anyone had ever done to her.

It was Gareth's dad who had seen Maddie's mom down by the harbor one night and then told Gareth about it. The next day, Gareth had told everyone else in their school.

What Gareth's dad was doing down there at night was something Maddie had often thought about asking him, to get back at him, but that was only when she thought about it afterward, lying at home in her bed. Once the teasing started, she never knew how to say anything. At least nothing clever. Fact was, she too was embarrassed by her mother's profession. She didn't even want to defend herself. Because if her mother was dirty like they said, then so was she.

Maddie sobbed a little more when she realized that her blindfold had slipped up slightly on the right side and light was coming in. It must have happened when she fell. She managed to push it further up by sliding across the carpet, and soon she could actually see something.

Maddie gasped as she looked around the barren room with nothing but the carpet she was lying on and strange black foam on the walls. There was only one other thing there. A huge wooden box was placed against the end wall. Maddie stared at it, and as she paid attention, she thought she could hear a noise coming from inside of it.

It sounded an awful lot like nails scratching against the wood.

Chapter 38

"WHAT'S THE RUSH?"

Matt got out of the police cruiser. I was standing in my driveway, where I had asked him to meet me.

"You said you owed me, remember?" I asked. "Big time, you said. I'm going to have to cash in on that right now."

It had taken me a couple of deep breaths to call for his help, but the fact was, a girl's life was on the line, and our little quarrel shouldn't be allowed to end up costing her life.

Matt gave me a look. It reminded me of how he used to look at me on the playground at school. It was a look that I never knew if he wanted to hit me or play with me.

He scratched his stubble. "Okay. What is it?"

"It needs to stay between us. You can't tell any of your colleagues."

"I…I don't know, Eva. It sounds like trouble."

"It is trouble, but a girl's life is depending on us," I said.

He wrinkled his forehead. "You're telling me you want me to help you do police work…illegally?"

I threw out my arms. "Not illegally. Just…bend the rules a little. Help me save a young girl."

He rolled his eyes at me. "You're going to be my death, Eva Rae Thomas. I always knew you would be."

I leaned over and smiled. "I'm counting on it. So…do I have your word? That you will keep this between you and me?"

He stared at me, contemplating, weighing the pros and cons, his nostrils flaring lightly.

"All right," he said. "But then we're even, you hear me?"

I exhaled, relieved. "Thank you."

I told him the story of Maddie and Mrs. Altman and the photo, while his eyes grew wider and wider.

"And she never told the police?" he asked with anger in his voice.

"No," I said. "She can't. She's a prostitute. She'll lose her daughter. DCF will take her."

"Darn right, she will. And she should. For leaving her alone at night," Matt argued. "No kid should be home alone all night."

"You and I can agree on that, but we can also agree that sometimes desperate times call for desperate measures, okay? This woman is trying her best. Besides, that's not the point here. The girl is in danger, and we can help her. Let's help a girl and her mother, okay?"

Matt looked at me. He was about to argue again but stopped himself as our eyes locked. I saw the softness in them that I remembered so well. He never could say no to me.

"All right," he said. "You said you know where she is?"

"I know who took her," I said. "And I think maybe he's the same one who took Sophie Williams. I did see a white car parked in the alley that night before she was found. It could be this one. You could end up solving your case. Not half bad, huh?"

"Okay, I'm buying into it. Who is he?"

"Thomas Price. Sophie Williams' coach."

I opened Mrs. Altman's photos on my phone and showed him.

"Here. This is his car that Maddie was picked up by. This is the last time she was seen. I had Cooper run the plate, and it belonged to Thomas Price."

He grabbed the phone and studied the picture, then nodded. "Cooper is involved too?"

"Just for running the plate. He doesn't know anything else."

Matt gave me a look, then sighed. "All right. Let's go have a chat with him."

Chapter 39

MATT HANDED me his Police jacket to put on while we walked up to the house.

"Just to make sure you look official," he said.

I nodded while putting it on. It felt strange to wear one again. Especially in this heat.

Matt smiled when he saw me wearing it.

"What?" I asked.

He shrugged. "It suits you."

"Very funny," I said as I walked up to the door and knocked. It took a few seconds before Thomas Price opened it. He stared at Matt, then at me, a look of confusion on his face.

"Officer Miller?" he asked. "What's going on?"

"We're looking for a girl," he said and showed him the picture of Maddie. "Madeleine Jones. Have you seen her around?"

He took a quick look, then shook his head. "Nope. Never seen her before."

"We have reason to believe she might be hiding some-where around here," I said. "Could we take a look around inside?"

Thomas Price shrugged. "I don't see why. She's not here."

The tone in his voice got angrier...almost hissing.

"We're not accusing you of anything, Mr. Price," I said. "We just need to take a quick look around."

He gave me a strange look. "Who is she, Matt? Why is she suddenly everywhere? I thought you had kids to take care of. Or was that just a lie you told me this morning? What is all this? Why are you harassing me?"

"I assure you, sir, I am not..." I said, but we had lost him. He shook his head violently.

"If you don't have a warrant, then you're not coming inside," he said.

"Thomas," Matt pleaded. "It's just a quick look around. If she's not there, we'll be out of here immediately."

"Why would she be here?" he asked aggressively. "You don't think I know what's in my house? You don't think I would know if a girl was inside my house?"

"She could be hiding, maybe under a bed or something," I said, thinking this was getting too far out. He was onto us, and there was no way we were getting inside that house.

"You know what? How about I take a look around myself and then I'll call you if I find a little girl, how about that, huh?" Thomas Price said. As he was about to slam the door shut, I put my foot in it to stop it. It hurt like crazy as he tried to close it anyway, but I didn't care. I pushed it open, pushed him aside, and rushed past him.

"Maddie?" I called, hurrying into the living room.

The TV was on but muted. The News was on, talking again about the senator's son. I turned away, then spotted a door and ran to open it. Thomas Price was yelling behind me, but I hurried, so he couldn't catch me. Matt was yelling at me to come back out too. Meanwhile, I rushed into the bedroom and looked around, but found nothing, not even in the closets that I pulled open. I then ran to another bedroom and looked around, even under the bed, but found nothing.

"Maddie!" I called, hoping she would hear me and answer, but there was nothing.

Thomas Price was now in the doorway, yelling at me to get the hell out of his house. I walked up to him, stared into his eyes, and felt a chill run down my spine as I saw the look in his.

"You can't just come in here," he growled. "I know my rights."

"Where is she?" I asked and showed him the picture of his car from my phone. "She got into your car."

Then Thomas Price started to laugh. "Did you see my car in the driveway?"

"No."

"I don't have a garage, and you assume I have the car somewhere? Where? In my living room?"

"What are you saying?" I asked.

He leaned over. I could smell his breath as he spoke. "I gave my car to my mom three weeks ago. She needs it more than I do since hers broke down. I can walk to the ocean from here. If I need to go further, I just pick it up at her place."

Matt came up behind him. I felt the blood leave my face.

"Embarrassing, huh, Officers?"

"You could still have borrowed it, and the car is part of an ongoing investigation," I said.

Coach Thomas shook his head. "You're crazy, lady. Now, please, get out of my house. I wonder what the chief is going to say when she hears about this. You know she and I go way back, right?"

Chapter 40

I LOOKED AT MATT. We were driving back in his cruiser. It was getting dark out, and bugs were dancing in the headlights. I felt terrible.

"I am so sorry," I said. "I was so certain she was there, you know with his connection to Sophie Williams and everything."

Matt sighed and stopped the cruiser outside my house. "You were only trying to help...I guess."

"I hope I didn't get you in trouble?" I asked.

"We'll see. But maybe...just maybe you should leave the police work to me from now on, okay?" he said, forcing a smile. "I know you used to be a big shot and everything, but maybe you need to focus on yourself and your family right now."

I grabbed the door handle, then opened the door before looking at him again.

"Thank you, Matt. I am glad you were here today. I'm just sad we didn't find the girl."

"Well, I did owe you one. But now we're even, okay?" he said. "I'll go talk to Price's mother before I head home today. Just to make sure the girl isn't over there, but I know her, and she's an old woman. Still, I'll check just to be certain. I'm sure that'll help you sleep better tonight."

I nodded. "Thanks."

I watched his cruiser as it disappeared down the road, then turned with a deep sigh and walked inside. I knew I wasn't supposed to do any more police work, but how could I not? Maddie was still out there somewhere, and her mother had put her confidence in me finding her.

Barely had I set my foot inside of the house before Olivia stood in front of me, hands on her sides, an angry look in her eyes.

Uh-oh.

"Where have you been?" she asked.

"I...I had to be somewhere, why? Is everything all right?" I grabbed my phone and looked at it—eleven calls and seven texts, all from Christine. My first thought was that something had happened to Alex, but as I finished the thought, I heard a loud scream coming from the stairs, and Alex came storming toward me, holding out a sword. I exhaled in relief. The boy was okay. Louder than ever, but okay. Then what was it?

"Is it Christine?" I asked, my heart beginning to race.

"You're darn right it is," Olivia said.

"What happened?" I asked, panic beginning to rush through me.

"You missed it," Olivia said.

"I missed what?" I asked. "Olivia, tell me what is going on right away. You're scaring me."

"Her concert," Alex screamed.

I looked at him then up at Olivia. "What concert?"

"Christine's concert. It was tonight," Olivia added.

"What concert? I never heard anything about a concert?" I asked, still feeling confused.

"Her choir concert," my daughter said. "She even put the note up on the fridge to remind you; look. You really mean to tell me you didn't know?"

I rushed to the fridge. There it was, right in the middle where I couldn't miss it.

How could I not have known this?

"So...where is she now?" I asked.

"She's still there. But it's too late to go," Olivia said. "The concert is over now. She'll be home soon."

"Oh, okay," I said, disappointed. "Guess I'll have to make my famous chili for dinner, huh? Her favorite." I was about to take out some meat when I paused. "Say...how did she get there? Did she bike?"

Olivia shook her head. "Nope. She got a ride from someone."

"She got a ride? From whom?" I asked.

Olivia shrugged. "How am I supposed to know that? Some parent, I guess."

Chapter 41

I WAS ABOUT to explode with anxiety for the next fifteen minutes. It felt like forever; that's how nervous I was. I couldn't stop thinking about Maddie Jones and the white car. What if Christine never came back? Just like Maddie had never come back?

I was terrified.

I called my parents and talked to my dad. My mom said she couldn't deal with this right now and gave the phone to my dad, who calmed me down. I told him about Maddie and how she had gotten into a car with a stranger and how I was so scared the same thing had happened to Christine. I told him how we had been on the trail of finding her, tracing the car, but had run into a dead end.

"I get why you're freaking out," he said. "Believe me; I do. There is nothing worse than not knowing where your kid is. But you have to remain calm. It won't help anything if you lose it. It won't bring her back. Give it time. She might be back."

After exactly fifteen minutes of me watching the driveway from my window, my stomach in knots, biting my nails, a car drove up the street, and I spotted my daughter in the window. The car slowed down to a stop, and she got out, then walked up to the house. I ran to the door, heart beating hard in my chest.

"Christine!"

I was about to take her in my arms, but she pulled away.

"Mom. How could you forget?"

"I am so sorry, baby, I am so, so sorry. I…I hadn't seen the note on the fridge. I know I should have but I didn't…and I was just so…scared."

She wrinkled her forehead. "You were scared? Why?"

"Christine. You went in a car with a complete stranger. What have I told you all your life about strangers?"

Christine stared at me. "You've got to be kidding me? You're making this about you again? Of course, you are. You're trying to make me feel bad when you're the one who screwed up? All the other parents were there. I was the only one whose mother wasn't there. Do you have any idea how that feels? I almost missed the entire concert because you weren't there to take me. I waited forever for you to come home. I called you a million times, but you didn't answer. I was about to go by bike, but I knew I would get there too late, when he came along. Luckily, he could take me, and I made it in time."

"Who?" I asked, my hands still shaking. "Who took you there?"

"His name is Phillip," she said. "He's the captain at the fire station. He was wearing his uniform. He said he knew you."

"And you went with him? In his car? Just like that?" I said, my heart thumping in my chest. After all the years I had spent telling my girls to be careful, I couldn't believe she could be so careless.

"Would you stop it? It's not like that," she said. "He was only trying to be nice. Besides, I'm back, aren't I? Nothing happened."

She was about to walk past me when I grabbed her arm.

"This time. Promise me you'll never do it again. Never get into a car with a stranger."

Christine looked at me, then rolled her eyes at me. "Mom, would you cut it out? I know something bad happened to you once. I know some guy tried to grab you in Wal-Mart; I know it happened to you, but it doesn't..."

"My sister was kidnapped, Christine. It wasn't just a little thing. It wasn't just me overreacting. I never saw Sydney again after that day. No one knows what happened to her. Not a day goes by when I don't wonder why the guy took her and not me."

Christine looked into my eyes, then exhaled. "I know this story, Mom. You've told it to me a thousand times. It doesn't mean the rest of us can't live our lives. Now, can I please go? I have homework to do."

I let go of her, and she ran up the stairs. I looked at my trembling hands. I walked into the kitchen and grabbed a bottle of wine, my hands shaking so heavily I could barely hit the glass when pouring it.

Chapter 42
THEN

THE BOY WAS DOWN in the living room when it happened. His dad had brought home a new toy truck for him, and he had woken up early on this Saturday to play with it. His baby sister came down too and brought her dolls with her, and now they were playing on the floor, blocking out the world and forgetting everything around them for just a few hours.

The knock on the door was loud and demanding. The boy gasped and looked at his sister when they both heard it. The boy swallowed, knowing he wasn't allowed to open the door when his dad and new mommy were sleeping. Still, the knocking continued, and the two children got curious.

Together, they walked to the window and peeked outside.

Baby sister gasped. "It's Momma!"

The boy's heart pounded, and he could hear his pulse in his ears. He didn't know what to do. Seeing his mother made him feel warm and happy, yet he knew he couldn't count on her. She could be high and then there was no telling what she might do. That was what his dad had told him. That was why they didn't go visit her anymore. Their dad was afraid of what she might do to them.

"We have to let her in; come," his baby sister said.

Mommy knocked again, hard and angrily. It frightened the boy. Soon, she was yelling too.

"Let me in! I want to see my children! Tommy, I know you're in there! TOMMY!"

His sister looked at him, pleading. "She wants to come in. She wants to see us; come."

His sister rushed to the door and reached for the handle. The boy stood like he was frozen.

"Wait," he said worriedly. "We should wake up Dad first."

"Why? She wants to come in. Let's let her in," baby sister said, tilting her head, not understanding. "It's Momma."

"No," the boy said and walked to her, grabbing her hand. "We can't."

His sister burst into tears. If there was one thing in this world the boy couldn't stand, it was his sister crying. It hurt his heart so badly he couldn't stand it.

"I want to see my momma!"

"Okay, okay," he ended up saying. He grabbed the lock and unlocked the door. His sister stopped crying and grabbed the door handle, then turned it and the door swung open.

Outside stood their mommy and, as he saw her, the boy's heart started to race. She smiled and bent down, holding out her arms.

"My babies!"

Baby sister ran to her and hugged her tightly, while the boy stayed behind scrutinizing his mother. She had gotten skinnier, her cheeks had sunken in, her eyes had deep dark marks beneath them, and she looked different. He didn't like the way she looked.

"Aren't you going to hug your mommy?" she asked.

The boy stared at her, contemplating for a few seconds more, then decided he would love to feel her embrace once more and took off toward her. He had barely reached her when a voice yelled from the stairs behind them.

"What's going on here?"

It was Daddy and New Mommy. They were storming down the stairs, barely dressed, New Mommy wearing a silky robe, daddy in his jammies. They grabbed baby sister and the boy and New Mommy pulled them inside, while Daddy started to yell. The boy heard it all from inside the house, while his sister cried her little heart out.

"You can't just come here like this."

"They're my children too, Tommy. I am entitled to see them."

"Look at you. You can't even look me in the eye. Look at how your hands are shaking, not to mention your slurred speech. You're high again, aren't you?"

"No! Why would you say that? Tommy?" their mommy pleaded. She was crying now, and the boy wasn't sure he could hold his tears back much longer either.

"Get off my property before I call the police. You hear me? I don't want to see you here."

"But...Tommy...they're my children...I want to see them," she cried. "How can you be so cruel?"

"Get out."

"I don't want to go," she said, hissing. "I'm not going till I have seen my children."

"Then I'll just have to call the cops then," their dad said.

"You can't steal them from me."

"Go home."

The boy looked out the door, just as his mother picked up a rock from the flowerbed, the one with the irises that New Mommy loved so much. His old mommy threw it at the window. The window shattered with a loud noise and both children screamed. Glass scattered everywhere in the living room. Outside, their mother was screaming too as their dad tackled her and pulled her into the street.

"Don't you ever come back here, or I'll make sure the police put out a restraining order," he yelled.

The boy grabbed his sister in his arms as their mother

walked away, head slumped, still yelling. Meanwhile, their father came back inside, snorted, then slammed the door behind him. He knelt by his children and pulled them into a warm embrace. Both kids were shaking heavily.

"What's wrong with Mommy, Daddy?" the boy asked, tears streaming across his cheeks.

"She's not well, son," he said.

"Can't a doctor make her well?" little sister asked, with a sniffle.

Their dad shook his head. "I'm afraid not."

"Why not?" the girl asked.

"She's a drug addict," the boy answered. "It can't be cured."

"I'm so sorry you had to see her like this," their dad whispered. "That's what drugs do to people. They make them act irrationally. Right now, your mother isn't acting rationally. You can't trust her. But I promise you, it won't happen again. I won't let it. I'll protect you."

Chapter 43

AFTER SAYING goodbye to the kids the next morning, I walked upstairs and opened my safe, then found my gun. When we moved to Cocoa Beach, I had put it away, thinking I wasn't going to get any use of it, but I wasn't feeling safe anymore, not even in my small cozy hometown. Maybe I was just being paranoid like my daughter said; I didn't know. But I knew this feeling a little too well, and I also knew that wearing a concealed gun made me feel safer.

I sighed and looked at my phone. I still wasn't convinced of Coach Thomas' innocence, to be honest, but at the same time, I found it hard to keep looking into him since it would only end up hurting Matt. I would have to tread carefully.

There was something, though, that I had to check. A thought that had entered my mind and I couldn't let go. I grabbed my computer and began a search, then found some old articles that I began to read. I made a few phone calls back to some old colleagues out west in California and made tons of notes on my pad. Then my dad called, and we chatted for about half an hour. As I hung up, there was a knock on my door. I walked to the window and looked down into my driveway.

It was Matt.

"What's he doing here?" I mumbled.

Probably came to yell at you for ruining his career.

I walked down and opened the door, preparing an entire speech of excuses but also ready to defend myself, when I took one glance at his face and realized that wasn't why he was here. This had nothing to do with what had happened the day before.

"We need to talk. Can I come in?"

"Of course," I said and stepped aside. He had his laptop under his arm, which he placed on my kitchen counter. He sat down on a stool with a deep sigh. There were cereal leftovers all over and spilled milk, which I hurried up and wiped away.

"You look like you could use a cup of coffee," I said.

"Yes, please." He tried to smile, but I knew him well enough to know that he was forcing it. He was biting his lip and, from the look of it, he had been at it all morning, maybe even all night.

I poured coffee for the both of us, then found some cookies and put them out, but Matt didn't touch them. Instead, he sipped his coffee, then looked deep into my eyes.

"What's going on, Matt? You're scaring me. Did something happen? Have you gotten in trouble with Chief Annie because of me?"

He rubbed his forehead. "Chief Annie sent me here. Not to scold you, but to beg you. It's time we bury the hatchet and face reality. We can't do this on our own. I've come to ask you to help us out with the case. We're in deep here. Too deep, Eva Rae. We need your help. Do you think you can do that? Chief Annie told me I had to get down on my knees and beg you if I needed to. Do I need to?"

I sat down on a stool next to him, completely taken aback, holding my coffee between my hands.

"I…I have…"

"I know you have this book to write," he interrupted me, "and that you're super busy with other stuff, but we can't do this without you. Things have gone from bad to worse since yesterday, and we simply don't have enough experience to deal with it. Please?"

I put my hand on his arm to stop him talking. "That's not what I was trying to say. I was about to say that I would love to. But I need to have free hands. I need to do this my way."

"Whatever it takes," Matt said. "Chief's orders. And I will behave too."

I chuckled. "Was that an excuse?"

"I guess. I was an idiot the other day. I'm sorry," he said. "You're allowed to flirt. I don't know why I got so mad."

"I get it," I said. "The pressure is on your shoulders. Now, show me what's on that computer. I don't assume you brought it to check your emails."

Chapter 44

"WHERE DO I BEGIN?" Matt said, his voice heavy. He had opened his laptop and was clicking the mouse. "Oh, yes. The autopsy. Let's begin there."

He opened a document, and I moved my stool closer, so I could look over his shoulder. He smelled just like he used to when we were younger. It brought back many fond memories and a sense of comfort to me.

"Sophie Williams died from asphyxiation, they concluded," he said.

"When?" I asked. "When was she strangled? She was taken three months before she was found, but the body wasn't decomposed."

"Oh, yes, well, time of death is set to be somewhere between eight p.m. and eleven p.m. on the night she was found, October 5th."

"Okay, so in other words, he kept her for three months somewhere before killing her and placing her there," I said. "What else? Was she abused sexually?"

He shook his head.

"Okay, so it's not something sexual, which I'm quite

surprised about, to be honest. She was dismembered; we saw that," I said. "Do they know with what tool?"

Matt nodded. He swallowed hard. "A sharp object, possibly an ax, it says."

I nodded again and sipped my coffee. "A common household tool. What has me rattled is the fact that he dismembered her but not to dispose of the parts. That's usually the reason for dismembering someone. To get rid of the parts one after another in order not to be discovered, but that's not this killer's motive. It's not the kill itself; it's the displaying of the victim that gets him going."

"Which leads me to the next part, the one that has us all puzzled."

I sipped more coffee, then looked at him. He looked like he needed a moment to prepare himself to be able to say what came next. I braced myself for something nasty.

"The body parts didn't belong to her," he said.

"Excuse me?"

He swallowed again. "The arms and legs weren't hers. The head and torso were."

It took a few seconds before the realization finally sunk in. I blinked a couple of times, then wrinkled my forehead.

"They weren't hers?"

He shook his head.

"Then whose were they?"

He tapped on his computer, and another file came up. A picture appeared of a young boy, looking to be about the same age as Sophie.

"Scott Paxton, also twelve years old, disappeared on Sunday, September 12th while biking home from a friend's house. He's from Titusville. His mom's a drug addict who didn't notify the police till several days had passed and then she told them she believed his dad had taken him. They put out an Amber Alert, but neither the dad nor the boy was ever found. In the end, they just assumed he had run away with him…maybe to another state."

"But he hadn't," I said and ran a hand through my hair while thinking about all this new information. The Cocoa Beach Police had done an excellent job of hiding this from the press. As soon as they found out, they would gobble it all up and spread panic in town. It was a good call to hide it for as long as they could. Especially since it seemed like the killer wanted this out; he wanted this part to be told, the gory details. I wasn't sure why yet, but there was no doubt that this was his goal. Otherwise, he wouldn't have gone to such trouble to do it and display the body the way he did. The more I got to know about this killer, the less I liked.

"There's more," Matt said.

"I had a feeling there was," I said and finished my cup. "Let me just get a refill first. I have a feeling I'm going to need a lot of caffeine for this."

Chapter 45

I REFILLED both of our cups and grabbed a cookie. I know that most people wouldn't be able to eat in the middle of something like this, but I wasn't like most people. I could always eat and, the more troubled I was, the more I did. Or maybe I just couldn't help myself. I needed some comfort in the middle of all this human tragedy and misery.

"So, last night, this came to our attention," Matt said. "Or rather it was sent to me directly, in an email addressed to me."

I leaned over and watched him open an email, then click on a link. The link sent him to YouTube where a video appeared. He started it and leaned back so I could see better.

At first, it showed a video of Sophie Williams from when she was still alive. She was sitting in a room, on the floor, tied up, her mouth duct-taped. She was crying and screaming behind the tape.

"Oh, dear Lord," I said.

"There's more," he said.

Another clip appeared, this time of the senator's son sitting in the room where we found him, money stuffed down his throat, gasping for air behind the bills.

Then there was text sliding across the screen, while the boy was groaning and gasping for air behind it.

DO I HAVE YOUR ATTENTION YET?

I glanced quickly at Matt next to me when he signaled for me to keep watching.

A new text appeared.

FACTS:

Every 36 seconds, there's one divorce in the U.S.

That's 2,400 divorces a day.

16,800 a week.

876,000 a year.

50 % of American children will go through their parents' divorce.

Children of divorce suffer in school.

They have behavioral problems.

They are less likely to graduate from high school.

Kids of divorce are more likely to commit a crime while juvenile.

They are five times more likely to live in poverty.

They suffer from health issues like anxiety and depression.

Their suicide rate is twice as high.

Even God hates divorce, Malachi 2:16

The text stopped, and the camera then zoomed in on the face of a crying Sophie Williams. And then the camera was turned off, and the screen went black.

I leaned back and stared at Matt, who was still very pale. I shook my head and scratched my forehead, then grabbed my phone and found my Bible app and read out loud from Malachi 2:16:

"'*For I hate divorce!' says the LORD, the God of Israel. 'To divorce your wife is to overwhelm her with cruelty,' says the LORD of Heaven's Armies. 'So guard your heart; do not be unfaithful to your wife.'"*

I put the phone down, wondering if I should send this passage to Chad. Matt gave me a look.

"You understand now why we need your help?" he asked.

I sipped my coffee while chewing on all this new information. I grabbed another cookie and bit into it. A couple of crumbs fell to the counter. I ate the cookie while thinking some more.

"So…what do you think?" Matt asked cautiously.

I spoke with my mouth full, lost in my thoughts. "First off, he placed the body for us to see, somewhere he knew tourists came, where everyone comes. He wants our attention. That's why he chose Sophie, a girl in the public eye. The same goes for the senator's son. He wants to make sure he's the talk of the town. That the media will talk about this. But not because he gets a thrill out of it; no, this runs deeper. He has some sort of mission with this. Now the part about dismembering the body and putting it together the way he did using parts from another child—also from a home of divorce—it symbolizes something for him. There's a message here for us to read. After seeing this video, there is no doubt. It represents the way children are split in a divorce. There's a split between parents, and sometimes siblings are split as well, torn apart in their loyalty and sometimes physically between two homes, two lives. I must say, it's very carefully created. He's put a lot of thought into this, which tells us he's extremely calculated and deliberate. This is well-planned beyond anything I have seen before."

Matt nodded, growing paler as I spoke. "And the senator's son?"

"The senator's son, and the money in his mouth, I will assume represents poverty. How children often end up in poor conditions after a divorce. Mothers who don't get alimony or just the loss of the extra income often sends children into a life of poverty."

"But the senator's son isn't poor?" Matt said.

"I know. That's what has me wondering a little. Wait a second. The place he was found. The old lady living next door said the place had been empty. Why was it empty?"

Matt sighed. "A colleague told me yesterday that there was a tragedy about three years ago. A woman was shot by her own son. He was sick, mentally ill and had been since his dad left them. She had been pleading for help from the county to handle him because she couldn't afford it for him."

"And so, he shot her. Poverty led to tragedy. Poverty after a divorce," I said, pointing at Matt. "Now...I have a feeling that Maddie Jones fits into this picture as well. As much as I don't want to, I feel like she is about to play her part in this twisted plan."

"How?"

"Her mother," I said. "After her parents divorced, she was forced into prostitution. Not an uncommon result in poorer neighborhoods. Now, Maddie must have felt shameful about her mother's profession."

"So, you're thinking she represents the guilt and shame that children who go through a divorce often suffer?"

I gave him a smile. "Exactly."

He leaned back in his stool. "Wow. So, you're telling me we're looking for a killer who is angry about divorce?"

I grabbed another cookie and dunked it in my coffee. "Yes. It must mean something to him, something profound."

"But...that could be anyone?"

I nodded and bit into the soaked cookie. "I know. He is highly intelligent. He is most likely a very well-functioning person, might have a family and children even. He probably even holds a steady job where he never takes any sick days, and his work is impeccable, and he is very likely part of your local community or has been at some point. Why else would he choose this place?"

"Yak."

"I know. The guy is highly delusional and thinks he's on some sort of mission. He might even think he's doing something good, like he's helping the world to be a better place. Those are some of the most dangerous killers you get. They see the flaws, but they also see the solution, and they're determined to let the world know. They want to fix us all."

"So, he's a…"

"He could also be a woman, just sayin'."

"Okay, so he or *she*…is a delusional psychopath trying to change the world? Working for the greater good? And his—or her—kills are inspired by how divorce affects children? A killer who targets children of divorce?"

I nodded. "And then the worst part."

Matt's eyes grew wide. "There's a worse part?"

I nodded. "I'm afraid so." I handed Matt a cookie for comfort. He took it with worried eyes.

I tilted my head with an exhale. "This is not his last kill."

Matt sighed resignedly. "I was afraid you might say something like that. There will be more?"

"Most likely, yes. I fear that he's just getting started. He has more planned for us. That's why he has taken Maddie."

Matt looked overwhelmed. I couldn't blame him. This was quite a lot to take in.

"So, what do we do next?"

I swallowed the rest of my cookie and looked at him. "First of all, did you get someone to trace the email?"

"The IT department is on it," Matt said. "I don't know how long it will take, though."

"Okay, good. Next, we need to find Maddie before it's too late. We start by making a list of possible suspects. On the top of mine is Coach Thomas Price. It was his car that she was seen getting into. That's where we begin. Can you tell me what his mother said last night? About the car?"

He nodded. "She didn't have it anymore. It was stolen from her driveway a week ago. At first, she thought it was just some kids who had taken it for a joyride. It had happened before several times with her old car. It would come back eventually smelling of weed. But when it didn't come back the first couple of days, she figured her son had taken it back. That he needed it for something. She's old and didn't really want to get involved with the police over an old car that she didn't use much anyway, so she never reported it."

"That sounds a little off to me," I said and made a mental note. "Plus, she's saying that her son still used it even though he gave it to her. If someone was trying to hide what they were up to, that would be a good way to do it. Hiding the car at your mother's, am I right?"

"Sure."

"All right. Is she divorced?"

Matt nodded. "As a matter of fact, she is. She was married twice, and neither of the marriages lasted."

"Could be a traumatic experience for a young boy, couldn't it? I say we take a closer look at him and put a search out for the car."

Matt nodded and grabbed his phone. "Got it."

As Matt walked out on the porch to call Cooper and have him do the search, I grabbed my phone and made a call of my own, following my strong hunch from earlier.

Chapter 46

MADDIE WAS WATCHING the box that was pushed up against the end wall. She had been staring at it for forever, listening to the scratching coming from inside of it. But there was one thing that worried her deeply. As the hours passed, the scratching grew lower, and soon it was very hard to hear.

Maddie wanted so badly to yell, to talk to the box, as she wondered if someone was actually inside of it or if it might be an animal of some sort. She thought at one point that she heard someone moan.

The blindfold was still pulled up on one side of her face, so she was able to gaze out a little bit from underneath it, just enough to take a look around. Not that there was much there to see. There was nothing on the floor except the carpet, and the walls were covered in some thick black stuff. The two windows were blocked by hurricane shutters that had been pulled down, and not much sunlight came in through the cracks. But it was enough for her to know when it was daylight outside and when it was nighttime, so she would know when to sleep. She also believed she heard an engine at some point and wondered if they were close to a road. She hadn't heard any other cars, though, so it had to be a small road.

Maddie lifted her head slightly, then turned around when she saw something she hadn't noticed before. On the wall. Someone had written something. By bending her legs and moving like a worm across the carpet, she squirmed closer and was able to look at it up close. By the bottom of the wall, where the black foam stopped, someone had scratched a word into the wood.

Sydney.

Maddie looked at it, then remembered she had known a girl named Sydney once. She had lived in her building. Had there been someone here who was also named that? Who was she? Had she been a prisoner too?

The thought made Maddie shiver as the realization sunk in. She wasn't the only one, was she? There had been others, others trapped in this room just like her. But what had happened to the other girls?

Maddie began to cry, and she couldn't stop it once she had started. Not till she heard fumbling behind the door and the key was put in the lock. Knowing what this meant, Maddie gasped behind the cloth, then fought to squirm her way back to her corner. She had been able to hide from her captor that she was able to look out beneath her blindfold. If she was found at the other end of the room, her captor would find out.

More fumbling as another lock was unlocked, then a hand on the door handle, and it turned.

Hurry up, Maddie!

Maddie squirmed and squirmed, her eye constantly on the door as it opened, and she slid into her corner just in time for her captor to enter. She whimpered and rolled up into a ball, but her captor didn't seem to care about her. Instead, the dark figure moved across the floor toward the box. Maddie was able to watch as the captor peeked inside the box, lifting the lid. A smile spread across her perpetrator's face, and there was a small whisper from their lips.

"You're ready. Just in time."

Chapter 47

"WE FOUND THE CAR."

"Already? That was fast," I said as I walked back to the kitchen. Matt had been waiting for me to finish my phone call, sitting patiently by his computer, his fingers tapping nervously on the counter.

"They just called from the station and said a state trooper found it on I95 on the side of the road."

"Ditched," I said. "Someone knows we're onto him and is getting rid of evidence."

"I'll have it checked for fingerprints," Matt said.

"Good. But don't expect to find anything, just like I wouldn't expect the IT guys to be able to track the email. This guy is too clever to be tracked. He won't leave any evidence behind."

"Chris is working with YouTube to get them to take the video down," Matt said. "Before anyone else sees it."

"Great. We need to keep it bottled up for as long as possible; if the media gets…"

There was an alarm on my phone, and I looked at the display. I had received a notification on Facebook from Melissa.

Have you seen this? She wrote.

I opened the post and saw the link. Then, my heart sank.

"It's too late. It's out," I said. "It's all over Facebook."

"What is?"

I turned my phone and showed him the video—the exact same one that had been emailed to him. Matt grew pale again.

"Oh, dear God."

I sighed. "It's already been shared more than three hundred times. I'd say you have about ten minutes before you'll have the entire press corps at your station, asking for answers. Even if you manage to get Facebook to remove it, it's still too late. The damage is done."

Matt found his cell again. "I better call the chief."

While Matt called her, my own phone vibrated in my hand, and I looked at the display. It was a call from California. I took it.

"Eva Rae?"

"Yes?"

"My name is Violet Dunn. You've been searching for me?"

I exhaled and walked to the living room, then sat down with my pad and a pen. "Yes, thank you so much for returning my call. I expect you know what this is regarding?"

"Agent Fisher filled me in, yes."

"So, what do you say?"

"I say we nail this bastard. I'm ready to talk."

I clenched my fist in victory.

"Great. Let's get to work. Why don't you tell me the entire story? From the beginning. Assume I don't know anything."

Chapter 48

THEN

THE BOY WAS DRESSED in a nice suit, and his dad was putting his tie on him, then he water-combed his hair.

"There. You look very handsome."

"Thanks, Dad."

His dad gave him a friendly pat on the shoulder. "Now, you remember what to say, right?"

The boy nodded, looking down at his feet. His dad saw it and grabbed him by the chin, then pulled his face up till their eyes met.

"It's okay, son. You're doing the right thing."

The boy nodded and held his dad's hand in his as they walked out to the car and drove through town. Neither the boy nor his sister spoke during the ride there. They stared out the window, wondering what state their mother would be in when they saw her.

Inside the courtroom, a lot of things were said that the boy didn't understand. He did get words like *long-term drug abuse, aggressive behavior, and unfit mother.* The rest seemed like a blur to him. But when it was his turn, and the judge asked him, the boy stood to his feet, cleared his throat, and said:

"That's right, sir. I want to live with my dad. I don't want to see my mother anymore."

The words fell like rocks from the sky. The boy's legs were shaking as he sat down again, feeling his sister's hand in his, squeezing it. Seconds later, it was her turn, and she did as she had been told.

"No, sir. I want to live with my daddy. I don't want to see my mom anymore. She hurts me."

Then, she sat back down, and they held hands again. They kept their eyes focused on their thighs and didn't lift their gaze to look at their mother, who was sitting at the table next to them.

Daddy and New Mommy had been very careful in telling them how to do this and not to cry. They knew it would be tough. They had told them it would, but it was for the best. This way, their dad could take care of them full-time and wouldn't have to send them to her when she was high and incapable of taking care of them.

They had been talking lots and lots about how it would go down in the courtroom, and they felt ready as they left the house, but nothing had prepared them for their mother's reaction.

The crying, the wailing, the screaming. It made the children lift their heads and look at the woman they no longer recognized as their mommy. She was yelling bad words, cursing at their father, screaming at them until someone stopped her and helped her sit back down.

Next to the boy, his sister started to sob, and he squeezed her hand once again to let her know he was there, and he was strong. He wasn't going to crack, even though he sensed how the knot in his stomach was growing so fast it threatened to burst.

Chapter 49

"WHAT ARE WE DOING HERE? You can't keep us here."

The words fell as Matt and I entered the interrogation room at Cocoa Beach Police Station. Thomas Price looked at us, then laughed.

"You two, of course. I should have known."

"What is this about?"

Jenna Williams was sitting next to him, looking more confused than ever.

"We just need to have a chat with you both; that's all," Matt said and held the chair for me so I could sit down. Matt was a gentleman to the bone. It simply was against his nature to let a woman sit down on a chair without holding it for her, just like he would never enter a door without holding it for a woman first. It was so deeply rooted in him that it was impossible for him not to.

Two of Matt's colleagues had brought Thomas Price and Jenna Williams in for us after I had hung up with Violet Dunn and the district attorney's office in Orange County, California. It was late afternoon now, but all the papers had been emailed to us, and now I was looking through them.

"Does Annie know what you two are up to?" Thomas Price asked. He looked at me.

I ignored his remark, then pulled out a picture of a girl and placed it in front of him. "You remember her?"

Thomas Price glanced at the photo with an indifferent attitude. "This is an old story."

"That's not what I asked," I said. "Do you recognize her?"

He shrugged "I don't know. Maybe."

"Well, let me help your memory. Her name is LeighAnn Dunn. She's the daughter of Violet and Peter Dunn. Peter Dunn was a photographer on the World Tour of Surfing at the same time you were a competitor, am I right?"

"Sure. I remember Peter." He looked at his watch. "Listen, could we get to the point here, please? I have a lesson in half an hour."

"You might be late for that," Matt said.

I smiled, then bobbed my head. "Yeah, you might be a little late."

Thomas Price slammed his hand on the table. "What the heck is this? Why are you harassing me at my home and now dragging me down here?"

"How's your back?" I asked.

He shook his head. "It's fine."

"I thought so. What can you tell us about LeighAnn?" I asked and pointed at the girl.

He exhaled and rubbed his forehead. He was getting sweaty now. "As I told you, it was a long time ago. It's not relevant anymore."

"Six years ago," I said and showed him the file. "It says here you were arrested for molesting her in Huntington Beach at a contest there when the girl was eleven."

He sighed again. Jenna let out a light shriek.

"Listen," he said. "The girl was nuts. She lied. The charges were dropped. If you did your research well, you'd know."

"I do know that," I said. "But today, I spoke with several

people, and lots of them aren't part of the WSL-tour anymore. And now they're ready to speak up. And they're telling me something funny. You know what they all told me? The same exact story, actually, which is kind of funny. At least I think so; you might not. But they all told me that the charges were dropped, but only because the WSL wanted them to be. They wanted to deal with it themselves. You had friends in high places, didn't you? They pulled the strings you needed. You were their wonder kid. A scandal like that might ruin the illusion. So, they made a deal. They told the Dunns to drop the charges and then you'd agree to drop off the tour. See, that was actually what made me wonder when I heard your story, and I went online to look into it. You were such a promising surfer. A huge talent and, suddenly, you dropped out and were never heard of again. The official story was that you had injured your back, but as I saw you the other day, doing airs and some pretty radical moves, I started to wonder if that was the entire truth. And that was when I started to ask around. A good friend of mine who works out of the FBI's LA office looked into you and found the old charges."

Thomas Price looked at me, then shrugged. "So what? As I said, it's an old story; the charges were dropped. Now, if you'll excuse me, I have to go help a kid achieve her dreams of becoming a professional surfer."

"The thing about child molesters is that they don't just stop," I said. "At least, not in my experience. They can cool down for a few years, being scared of being caught maybe, but the urge is still there. It never goes away. It nags inside them and refuses to let them go until they give in. And then one day, they slip up. They give in, just for a little…just one time."

"And then that time becomes a second time, then a third," Matt said.

I pulled out an evidence bag with Sophie's bloody underwear and put it on the table.

"And then one day it starts over again. Someone discovers what you're up to and the police get involved. You're back to being scared again."

"The blood proves nothing. She's twelve. She could have had her period," Thomas Price said.

"But she didn't," I said. "Jenna thought so too, so she took her to a gynecologist, who alerted her that this wasn't menstrual blood. She also told her that Sophie was training on way too hard of a level to have her period yet, right Jenna? She wasn't developed at all. That's when you got suspicious, right?"

"You thought it was your husband, didn't you?" Matt said, addressed to her. "At first, when the gynecologist told you her concerns. So, you wanted to divorce him. But when you realized it was Thomas, your daughter's esteemed coach, the one whose hands you had put your child's entire future in, you revoked the charges. And then you shut up like a clam."

Jenna started to cry now. She bent her head down. "I confronted him, but he told me if I ever told anyone, he wouldn't train Sophie anymore. She would never amount to anything. I knew he was right. He's the only trainer around here good enough to take her to the top. It was her future. It was her dream."

"And your dream as well," I said. "You couldn't risk it being shattered over such a small thing, could you?"

"Exactly," she said.

I exhaled and leaned back in the chair. "So, you just decided to close your eyes to the fact that your daughter was being molested. To pretend like it wasn't happening. She trusted you. You were the adult. You were the one who was supposed to protect her. And then, every freaking day, you sent her right back into the arms of the man who molested her, the very one who hurt her. How? How does anyone do that to...your own child?"

I felt Matt's hand on my shoulder.

"I've heard enough," he said.

I nodded and gathered my files. "Me too." I rose to my feet and put my chair back in place, then walked out, Matt holding the door for me.

"What happens next?" he asked.

"The California District Attorney's Office is gathering evidence to reopen the case against Thomas Price," I said. "The parents are ready to come forward and press charges, and they say there are others too. I'm pretty sure Jenna is willing to tell her story as well, so that should be enough to put the bastard down for a long time. FBI's Orange County office will take over now. One of my old colleagues works in that office. The statute of limitations for child molestation in California is ten years after the child turns eighteen, so that shouldn't be a problem."

Matt nodded, and we walked to his desk. They had cleared the desk across from his for me to use while I was working on this case as a consultant. Barely had we sat down before Cooper came in, looking perplexed.

"We didn't find anything. Not in his house or garage or at his mother's place. No sign of Maddie Jones or that any of the others have been there."

"Because he's not our killer," I said. "Thomas Price is just a child molester. This guy we're chasing is a mastermind. He's highly intelligent. Thomas Price is not. Besides, Sophie wasn't sexually abused when we found her. As I said, that is not what turns him on."

"So, what do we do next?" Chris Cooper asked. "All of our leads are gone. The car had no fingerprints, the email couldn't be traced, neither could the Facebook post. People and the press are gathering in the lobby, asking for answers. We don't have any?"

"We get some," I said and opened my laptop that I had brought with me. "And fast. Maddie Jones is still out there and hopefully still alive."

Chapter 50

THEY CALLED from the Apple store, and I drove down there to pick up Christine's computer right before they closed. It cost a fortune to get it fixed, but I knew just how happy my girl was going to be, so I paid up and drove back home.

As I walked inside, I stumbled over a fire truck. I could hear the kids upstairs and, as the door slammed shut, Alex screamed at the top of his lungs, then jumped down the stairs and threw himself into my arms.

"Mommy!"

Christine came down after him, yelling his name. "You clean up the mess you made in my room, immediately!"

She spotted me, then sighed. I had called earlier and had my dad come over and look after the kids while I was gone. I didn't want them to be alone all afternoon.

"Oh, good, you're home," she said.

I held out the computer toward her, and her eyes grew wide. "It's fixed? You fixed it?"

I nodded victoriously, taking full credit as if I had actually fixed it myself. I handed it to my daughter, and her face lit up. She threw her arms around my neck.

"You're the best mom ever."

"You're very welcome," I said and kissed her cheek, smelling her hair. I couldn't stop thinking about that girl LeighAnn and wondering who else Thomas Price had put his nasty fingers on. For once, I felt like I had made an actual difference, and my daughter had just called me the best mom ever. That called for a glass of wine and putting my feet up. In the kitchen, I found pizza and grabbed a piece. I also found my dad at the dining table, working on his laptop.

"I thought I heard your voice," he said.

I hugged him. I liked feeling his strong arms around me. My dad had always been in good shape and still ran several times a week on the beach. I was lucky that my parents were young when they had me, and I had always been grateful for that. I hoped to keep them around for a very long time. Even though my mom often made me want to scream. They were still my parents.

"So, what are you working on?" I asked. "I thought the markets were closed now?"

"There are always deals to be made," he said, "emails to answer."

"An investment banker never sleeps, huh?" I sipped my wine.

"I guess not," he chuckled and looked at me. "So, how was your day? Did you catch your killer?"

I sipped my wine again and took a bite of pizza. "We caught a bad guy, yes. But he wasn't the guy we were looking for."

My dad nodded pensively. "I never liked that Thomas Price. That's who it was, right?"

"I am not at liberty to say," I said. "You know, ongoing investigation and all that."

He laughed. "You don't have to. I met Mrs. Weiner outside of Tiny Turtle earlier. She's Thomas's neighbor. She told me Thomas had been taken in, and Jenna too. She assumed it had to do with the murder of little Sophie."

I scoffed. "Nothing gets past you, huh?"

"Nope. It's all anyone talks about these days. Especially with the video and all that. It creeps them all out."

"It wasn't Thomas, but we'll catch the right guy. Don't worry," I said.

"I'm not worried; well, that's not entirely true. I am worried about you. It's *we* now? You're working the case?"

I nodded. "They can't do this alone. This guy is seriously deranged. And clever."

"Just make sure you take care of yourself," he said with a deep sigh. "A guy this clever can also be dangerous, remember?"

"I'll be fine," I said. "Don't worry so much."

He shook his head, then reached over for a piece of the pizza with a smile. "Don't tell your mom."

"I'm not usually in the habit of sharing secrets with her anyway," I said.

He sighed and sunk his teeth into the cheese. "It's not getting better, is it?"

I shook my head. "Why is she being like that, Dad?"

"You know your mom. It's been tough for her...ever since...you know," he said. "She was never really herself again. It broke her."

"Why can't we even talk about it?" I asked. "We never did. It was like we just decided never to mention Sydney again. Like she never existed."

My dad exhaled and put the pizza down. "It was just easier that way, I guess."

I nodded and drank my wine, thinking about that day at Wal-Mart when that man had grabbed first me then my sister. I could barely remember what she looked like anymore. I had been so young. My mom had always resented me for not being able to remember anything, and for being the one he didn't take. I couldn't blame her. I felt guilty about that too.

"Well, I should get going," my dad said and rose to his

feet. He leaned over with his laptop under his arm and kissed my forehead. "Remember to take care of your family first. That's why you came down here. Don't you forget that. Enjoy every second you have with them. They won't be around forever."

Chapter 51

THE DARKNESS at nighttime was the worst part. Maddie hated when she sensed the lights go out of the room and darkness fall upon them. She knew another day had passed, another day she had spent in captivity, another day when she didn't get to see her mother or even the outside again. Oh, how she missed the fresh air.

They must be looking for me by now, right?

She sure hoped and prayed they were. She knew her mother would be, but she didn't know if her mother had returned home yet and discovered that Maddie wasn't there anymore. She could sometimes be gone for days. It could be like that time when she had ended up in the hospital and stayed there for four days before they let her go home. Her mother had told no one that she had a daughter at home, and she had been unconscious for days on end, she later told her, when Maddie was crying and asking where she had been for so long. It could be like that time, so maybe she hadn't found out that Maddie was missing yet.

Maddie had gotten some food. Earlier in the day, her captor had come into the room and had taken the cloth out of her mouth, ripping the tape off first. She had felt water splash into her mouth and bread hit her lips, and she was told to eat. So, she did. Greedily, she chewed on the old bread like it was the finest delicacy in the world. Never had bread tasted better, she thought as her stomach rumbled for more. But no more came. Her captor gave her more water, then put the cloth back in her mouth, Maddie pleading with him not to while he was taping it shut. Then she put her cheek back down on the carpet till her captor was gone again.

Now, as the darkness descended, she started to wiggle toward the box. Experience had told her that the nights were usually quiet. Her captor didn't come around at night, usually only once a day as far as she knew.

Maddie wormed her way to the box, then put her ear against it. There was a light scraping against the wood coming from inside of it. Maddie wiggled herself around so her back faced the box, then leaned her tied up hands against the box, reached out with her fingers as best she could and scratched the wood with her nails.

Then she stopped and listened. A few seconds later, there was a response. More scratching from the other side, this time louder and steadier.

Maddie laughed behind the cloth, then scraped the box again rhythmically. The scratching was repeated from inside the box.

I knew it! It's not an animal. No animal could repeat it exactly like that. This has to be a person. A real person, a human. I am not alone. Someone else is in here with me!

Up until now, Maddie had debated whether it was mice or rats maybe that she heard, but she had a feeling it was more than that, and now it was confirmed. Maddie wasn't alone.

She smiled behind the tape, then scratched the box again to let this person know she was there, and they weren't alone. The person returned her gesture, and they continued like that for a very long time until Maddie felt so exhausted she couldn't keep her eyes open behind the blindfold anymore.

Knowing she had to get back to her corner, she wormed her way back across the room, this time with a feeling of hope emerging inside of her. Not only wasn't she alone in this awful place, her chances of someone looking for her—for them—had just doubled.

Chapter 52

THE FACELESS MAN *is screaming and yelling because I bit his finger. Sydney is standing in front of us, dolls in her hands, as the man hisses at me. My mom has turned her cart around and sees us now.*

"Help!" I scream.

"Hey!" my mom yells, panic in her voice. She runs toward us. The man sees her, then gives me a short glare. I can see that he is panicking. He doesn't know what to do. That's when I notice his eyes for the first time. They're blue.

"Stop!" my mom yells. "What are you doing?"

The faceless man reaches out toward me, and I scream. Confused, he turns around and grabs Sydney instead. He holds her with his hand over her mouth and drags her away. She drops both dolls to the floor. I'm screaming; in the distance, I can hear my mom yelling. My heart is throbbing loudly in my chest as I watch the faceless man drag my sister out toward the entrance, my mom storming after him. I watch as he carries the screaming Sydney out of the store, where a white van waits for him, engine running.

The last thing I hear is my mom's heartbreaking screams, and then the engine roaring as the van takes off.

• • •

I woke up with a start. It wasn't the dream that woke me up; it was something else. A noise, I realized as I came back to myself. It was my phone; it was glowing in the darkness and vibrating. I looked at it. It was Melissa.

"What's going on?"

"It's Dawn," she said. "She's in the hospital."

I jolted upright. "What happened?"

"He beat her up."

"Oh, no, is she all right?" I asked.

"I...I don't know. I just got the call from her mother, and then I called you."

I sprang to my feet. "I'll pick you up in two minutes. Be ready."

I walked into Olivia's room and woke her up, telling her what had happened and that I needed to be gone for a few hours.

"It's okay, Mom," she said and kissed me. "You do what you have to do."

Neither of us spoke in the car while driving down Minutemen Causeway. As we reached A1A, Melissa sobbed.

"I knew he was bad for her, you know?"

I nodded. "He just seemed so nice."

"They all do," she said. "But she has a talent for finding them in a crowd. It's like she's drawn to them somehow. She only finds the true psychopaths, the ones who have everyone fooled."

I drove up in front of Cape Canaveral Hospital and parked the minivan. My heart was aching for Dawn as we took the elevator up to her room and walked inside. Her mom was sitting by her side when we entered. She stood to her feet. I remembered her from my childhood. A small woman who—just like Dawn—seemed to carry the weight of the world on her shoulders, but she was doing everything in her power to hide it.

"Melissa, and...Eva Rae? Is that you, girl?"

I nodded and hugged Dawn's mother. I could feel the bones in her body and feared I might crush her as I put my arms around her.

"How's she doing?" I asked. I looked at Dawn on the bed. Her face was almost unrecognizable. It was painful to see. Melissa burst into tears when she saw her. It was tough not to follow.

"She's sleeping now," her mother said. "They gave her something. She couldn't find rest."

We went to get some coffee and waited by her side for a couple of hours, sleeping in chairs, curled up uncomfortably. The night there gave me lots of time to think while looking out over the Banana River that the hospital faced. In the distance, I could see the lights from the cruise ships docked in Cape Canaveral while I thought about the case. It had brought so many memories up in my life that I could hardly sleep anyway. I kept thinking about Sydney and what had happened back then. I remembered how devastated I was, especially when I couldn't talk to my parents about what had happened. I just remembered the house suddenly going so quiet. It was like we stopped talking altogether. And laughing. There was no more laughter in my childhood home, where there had been so much before. Sydney had been the funny one, the one who always kept the rest of us happy.

I sipped my coffee in the hospital room, wondering what she would look like now if she were still alive. I remembered thinking I saw her everywhere in the days afterward. So often, I was certain it was her, but of course, it wasn't. It was just my imagination. She was gone and probably dead. Still, I never could stop wondering. What if she was still around? Every now and then, I would still think I saw her in a crowd.

"Mom?"

Dawn woke up. She blinked her eyes, and we went over to her. "Eva? Is that you?"

I grabbed her hand in mine and squeezed it. "We're going

to nail that bastard for what he did to you. I'm going to talk to Matt as soon as it is morning, and he'll..."

"Stop," Dawn said and shook her head.

"What?"

"I don't want you to make a big deal about this," she said. "Phillip is a nice guy. He's just...well, I'm the one who..."

"Don't you even dare go there," I protested. "This can never be your fault. Never."

"Eva Rae is right," Melissa said, wiping tears from her eyes. "You shouldn't let him get away with this."

"He's been through so much," Dawn said. "His ex-wife left him just two months ago. Took the kid with her. He just misses his daughter. That's all. It was his night off. I was drunk; we both were and then...we got into a stupid fight. I said something about him probably being the one who pushed his ex away and that was why she left. He couldn't take that. So, he hit me. Please, just leave him alone."

I looked at her, shaking my head. "I can't believe you. He does this to you, and you're...you're making excuses for him?"

"He's not a bad guy, Eva Rae," Dawn said. "I just have to be more careful what I say to him. That's all."

I left the room angrily. Melissa ran out after me. "Eva Rae, don't."

I stopped. I couldn't hold the tears back anymore, and now they were rolling down my cheeks.

"I can't just...I can't just..."

She grabbed my hand. "If she doesn't want to press charges, then that's her choice," she said. "You can't force her. You have to let it go."

"I'm going to freakin' kill that guy," I said.

"She won't press charges," Melissa said. "It's how it always goes. We can't change her, Eva Rae."

"What the heck happened to her? She used to be so strong?" I asked through tears.

"You also remember her dad, right?" Melissa said.

"Of course, how could I forget?"

"So, you remember how he treated her and her mother like dirt. All of Dawn's life while growing up. She would come to school with bruises, always on her body so no one would notice except her closest friends. Now, she's doing it to herself. How many times do you think I've been out here with her like this? It happens all the time. And, every time, she says she will stop seeing the guy, but next thing, she's back with him again. Or she finds someone new just like him. She can't help herself."

I wiped away the tears with my hand. "Maybe she can't stop it. But I can."

"Eva Rae, I don't like that look in your eyes," she said as I turned around and walked away. "What are you going to do, Eva Rae? Eva Rae?"

Chapter 53

I DROVE down my street and continued past my house. Two houses down, I parked and shut off the engine. Wild rage still rushing through my veins, I walked up to his door and knocked.

It took a few minutes before the light was turned on inside and someone came to the door. It was him. His hair was tousled, and his face bore marks from sleeping.

"Eva Rae? What...?"

"You sick bastard," I said, then clenched my fist and placed a punch right on his nose. His nose made a loud cracking noise as it met my knuckles. Phillip screamed and bent forward.

"What the...? What are you doing?" he yelled. He held a hand to his nose, and it came back with blood on it.

"That was for Dawn," I said, then turned on my heel and walked away. I could still hear him yelling at me as I started up the car and backed all the way down to my own house and went inside.

Once inside, I found some ice and applied it to my pounding knuckles, then sat down by the kitchen table with a deep sigh. I knew I wouldn't be able to sleep, so instead, I grabbed my laptop and opened the lid.

I entered the station's database, then opened Sophie Williams' case and went through all the files, going through every little detail of her disappearance from the Girl Scout camp. I wasn't quite sure what I was looking for, but anything that would stand out, anything no one had noticed before.

Except there wasn't anything. The leader, Michaela Strong had been interviewed over and over again about the last hours before the girl disappeared. She was also the one who had found out that Sophie was no longer in her tent when she came to wake her up the next morning. She had started the search in the woods afterward. She had called the police. For a very long time, they believed Sophie had walked out at night and gotten herself into the swamps and drowned. They had searched the river and swamps nearby for days afterward, using helicopters and airboats, but found nothing. The dogs hadn't been able to pick up a trace either. They had found nothing, not even a shoe or a piece of her clothing. Her sleeping bag had been gone with her, and that was what puzzled the investigation team. If she had wandered off, why bring the sleeping bag? If she were kidnapped, why would the perpetrator take it with him? It made no sense to them. Until now.

He placed her there in her sleeping bag for us to unwrap her, like a freakin' Christmas present.

I sighed and leaned back in my chair, running a hand through my hair. My eyes fell on the stacks of books and research files I had left out in the hope that I might one day get a little time to write my book. I wondered if I ever would. I had to, at some point, find the time. It was my bread and butter now. I had a deadline.

I grabbed one of the books and flipped a few pages, wondering about this Phillip character. He rubbed me the wrong way and had from the first time I met him. Why had he given Christine a ride the other day? I had met him once, and then he believed he could just drive around with my daughter? His car had been white too, like the one I saw at night in the alley, and like the one we saw in the picture. I hadn't taken a look at the license plate when he dropped off Christine. I should have paid more attention. That would have told me if it was the same one that picked up Maddie. He could have stolen it from Thomas Price's mother's driveway. It would be easy, and it would drive the suspicions elsewhere. Maybe that's what he wanted all along? To get us to focus on Coach Thomas so he could continue his mission on his own. Was it possible? Could Phillip be the killer? Was he sending me a message by taking my daughter for a ride? To let me know he could get to me at any time he wished? Get to the ones I loved?

He's too perfect, were Melissa's words. Could she be right? He sure fit the profile. He'd just gone through a difficult divorce too.

My eyes returned to the screen while a million thoughts rushed through my mind. Did Phillip Anderson know Sophie Williams from somewhere? I looked through the files and found his name on the search team along with the rest of the firefighters from our local station. They had pitched in and helped where they could, of course they had. Everyone did that around here, so nothing suspicious about that.

My head was spinning out of control. I opened Google and searched for articles about Sophie's disappearance and found hundreds in *Florida Today* alone. I spent the next several hours reading through them all until daybreak came and the sun began to rise outside my window. When the alarm rang on my phone, I laid my eyes on a picture in one of the later articles, an interview with Michaela Strong, the leader. As I stared at the picture, my heart started to pound heavily in my chest.

There it was; staring right back at me from the newspaper clip was what I had been looking for.

Chapter 54

"ARE YOU INSANE?"

Matt stared at me as I entered the police station and walked up to my desk. The place smelled of freshly brewed coffee. I needed that. I had fought with the kids all morning to get them to school on time. Christine had ended up yelling at me that she hated me. So much for best mom ever. Guess that was already forgotten by now.

"And a good morning to you too," I said and put my laptop down. I sat on my chair.

He came closer and leaned in over me. "You punched Phillip Anderson last night?"

"Oh, that, well...yes."

He shook his head and threw out his arms. "Are you crazy?"

"You already asked me that once," I said. "But to answer, no."

"He was in here earlier, blabbing on about how you came to his house in the middle of the night and punched him in the nose. The chief was furious. Why, Eva Rae? Why would you do that?"

"He deserved it."

A furrow appeared between his eyebrows. "I don't get you. He was threatening to press charges and everything. You're lucky you have me. I managed to talk him out of it."

"Let him," I said.

"What?"

"Let him press charges. I'll show the judge the pictures of the woman that he beat senseless last night."

Matt pulled out his own chair and sat down. "What are you talking about? Phillip? He would never do anything like that."

"Oh, I have the pictures to prove otherwise," I said and grabbed my phone. I found a series of pictures I had taken of Dawn while she was sleeping, just in case we needed them for prosecution later. I was still hoping she would change her mind and press charges against this guy.

Matt grabbed my phone and looked through them, swiping with small light gasps emerging from between his lips.

"In case you can't tell, that's Dawn. What's left of her."

"Phillip did this?"

I nodded.

"Oh, the bastard, I have never..." He looked up, and our eyes met. "He's such a nice guy?"

"They're usually the worst," I said, thinking about Chad and how wonderful he had been when we first met. He had never laid a hand on me; that wasn't his style, but he had turned around completely and showed a side to himself I didn't know existed. I could never have imagined he would abandon his children like that and not want to be with them anymore. Just like that. Had anyone told me six months ago, I would have laughed. Those kids were his entire life. I thought I knew him, but apparently, I had no clue.

"Wow, I must say, I am...baffled."

"Yeah, well...I have more," I said. "I've been looking into our little friend Phillip a little and guess what I found?"

"I have a feeling I'm not going to like this," he said.

I pulled out a print of the article and pushed it toward him. Matt looked at it, then back at me.

"So?"

"His ex-wife is Michaela Strong," I said. "And there's more. He was there. At the camp on the day Sophie disappeared."

"Okay, just as you were about to make sense, you go full-blown crazy on me again," Matt said. "What are you suggesting? He was there in the afternoon, yes, to talk about fire safety. His wife had asked him to. He does that all the time. He talks at the school every year too."

"But he was there on the day she disappeared. He stayed the night too. At the camp."

"With his wife and daughter, who was also part of the Girl Scout camp," he said. "It's perfectly normal. We were actually very happy he was there, so he could help with the search from the beginning and take charge of the situation. It could have ended in terrible chaos. He and his wife stayed on top of it from the beginning."

"Okay, but there's more," I said.

"Of course, there is," Matt said. He looked at me with a sly smile, like he was enjoying this. I ignored him and slid another piece of paper toward him.

"Have you been up all night or something?" he asked.

"Something like that," I said. "Read."

"What am I looking at here?" he asked. "Can't you just tell me and save some time?"

"Okay," I said. "I did a little search on Phillip in the newspaper's database, and this came up. This is a picture of Phillip with the senator's son from last year's Christmas parade."

"I can see what it is," Matt said, "but why is it important?"

"They knew each other," I said.

"This is Cocoa Beach; everyone knows each other."

"Okay, but there is one last thing that I found," I said.

"I can't wait to hear what it is," he said. He was starting to annoy me, but I did my best to ignore him.

"Maddie Jones," I said.

"Let me guess, he knew her too?" Matt asked.

"I called her mother this morning after driving the kids to school because Alex missed the bus again. She went to high school with Phillip up in Daytona. Before she was divorced, they lived not far from one another, and their girls used to play together when they were younger."

I looked at Matt. He shrugged. "So what?"

"Don't you see? He's connected to all three children?" I asked.

"So what? It's Cocoa Beach. We're all connected in one way or another. That doesn't prove anything."

"I know it doesn't, but it creates a connection. And that's all I need to get suspicious. The guy fits the profile like a glove. I'm sure if I dig a little deeper, I'll find more, something we can actually use against him."

Matt leaned back and crossed his arms over his chest with a sigh.

"What?"

"Listen, I get it. You want to nail this guy for what he did to Dawn; heck I want him punished for that too, but that doesn't mean he's our killer."

I nodded, knowing he was right. I couldn't let myself be blinded by my desire to get justice for Dawn.

"True," I said. "But it doesn't mean he didn't do it either. Besides, right now he's our only lead so far, so I say we go with it."

Matt sighed, then rose to his feet. "I'll get us some coffee."

Chapter 55
THEN

AFTER THE COURT had given their dad full custody, they moved to another part of town. The boy liked it there. His father built a playhouse in the treetop, and the boy spent many afternoons up there in that place that he had all to himself because his sister was busy swinging on the new swing set that their dad had put up for them.

New Mommy got a big bump on her stomach, and soon they were blessed with another sister, one who cried a lot at night, but otherwise brought much joy to the family.

As the years passed, the boy almost forgot about his mother, even though he sometimes sat in his tree house and cried about her. But he never told that to anyone. That was his little secret and the treehouse his hideout, where he could think about her and cry if he needed to without anyone seeing it.

He was angry with his mother for choosing the life she had and for not wanting him like his dad said she didn't. Instead, she had chosen a life of drugs and drinking and being a stripper. Hearing him talk about The Thing and how she lived her life made the boy feel ugly and dirty. His mother didn't even call on birthdays and, by the time the boy was a teenager, he resented his mother and he decided she was dead to him. He decided he might as well pretend like she didn't exist.

One day, as they were crossing the street and he was holding his sister's hand on their way home from school, there was a sudden yelling of his name. He recognized the voice, and the boy knew very well that it was her.

He didn't turn and look, but pulled his sister's arm to cross the street, but hesitated for just a second as his mother yelled their names once again. As he paused, the light changed, and he could no longer cross. This meant their mother could catch up to them.

"Hi, baby; hi, sweetie," she said, panting from running.

The boy didn't even look at her. He kept his eyes focused on the light and kept himself ready to rush across the street as soon as it changed. He held his sister close.

"Oh, my God," his mother said, clasping her face with her hands. "You've both grown so much."

She reached out her hands and felt his face. The boy pulled away, still without looking straight at her.

"Oh, my babies," his mother said, sobbing loudly now. "I can't believe it. Do you live nearby? I know your dad moved you. Is it close to here? Oh, it's so wonderful…I am so happy to see you both."

As she spoke, the light changed, and the boy pulled his sister's arm forcefully, saying:

"We're not happy to see you."

With those words he walked away, pulling his sister hard, still maintaining his posture and not letting even one tear escape the corner of his eyes. He wasn't going to give her the pleasure of seeing that.

Chapter 56

EVER SINCE THE BREAK-IN, Mary hadn't been sleeping well. It had happened three weeks ago but still gave her the chills, especially at night when everything was so quiet. It was on nights like these that she wished Don was still there with her. He had left her when the kids were one and three years old. Right when it got really tough, he had simply left and not looked back. Mary knew she too played her part in him leaving. She didn't fool herself and say she was the innocent one. She hadn't been herself since the birth of their second child. A depression her doctor had later told her it was. Postpartum. But at first, she didn't know what it was. It had knocked her out completely. For months, it was like she walked in a haze like she couldn't cope with anything in life, especially not a young child crying all night. And that was when she started taking it out on Don. He was the one who had worked all day to support them and, as soon as he came home, she couldn't help herself. She had to unload. At first, it was because she wanted him to feel sorry for her, to know that she too had a rough day, that she felt inadequate and guilty for not feeling all oozy and happy at the arrival of a new child. But when he hadn't been understanding the way she wanted him to, when he hadn't said the right things, and instead told her she was lucky that she got to stay at home, that was when she started to resent him. Mostly, she probably resented herself for not enjoying staying at home with the children like her mother had when she was a child. It was all Mary had ever dreamt of when growing up. Like her friends, she didn't dream of some big career. She just simply wanted to be a mother. But once the kids, Rylan and Faith, arrived, it had been nothing like what she wanted, what she thought it would be. Instead of feeling fulfilled, she had felt inadequate. She had this constant feeling of not being enough nagging inside of her, and this voice in her mind telling her she was doing it all wrong, that she was not cut out to be a mother, that she would end up destroying her children.

The yelling was bad, but it wasn't what drove him away. It was when the yelling stopped. Realizing it did her no good, that nothing in this world could make her feel better, Mary simply gave up. She dragged herself out of bed in the mornings and only did what was most necessary until she could crawl back into bed. Soon, she didn't even leave the bed at all.

Don begged her to talk to someone, to go to a doctor, but she didn't want to. She couldn't deal with the guilt that would ram her if she explained to someone from the outside that she couldn't even cope with her children, if she had to tell him how she had neglected her own children. She simply couldn't face that conversation.

So, she stayed in bed, and one day, Don didn't come home from work. He stayed out all night, and after three days, he finally came home...drunk. He told her he couldn't take anymore, that he had taken a job in Louisiana and he and a buddy were going up there the very next day.

Mary hadn't even asked him to stay. She had barely looked at him, and Don had left crying, slamming the door behind him. The divorce papers came with the mail a few days later when Mary had finally managed to get up and take care of her children. She realized she was all alone down here in Florida since all of her family lived up in North Carolina. It was after a phone call from her mother that she finally got herself to a doctor, who gave her the diagnosis and some medicine. Now she was doing a lot better and so were the kids. She didn't even miss Don, to be honest. Or all the fighting. It was actually better now that she was all alone. Don sent a check every month for them, and they lived decently.

The break-in had happened a few weeks ago. It wasn't so much the fact that there had been someone in her apartment; that was bad, yes, but the worst part was that it happened in the middle of the night, while Mary and the kids were asleep.

When they woke up the next day, the window facing the street was open, and there were dirty footprints on the carpet. Luckily, nothing had been taken, and the police told Mary that it was probably just some homeless person looking for shelter, thinking there was no one home, and then when he realized they were there, he had left.

Mary had believed them but still felt uneasy in her own bedroom. So it was again this evening when she had put the children to bed, and she lay in her bed, waiting for sleep to overpower her. She couldn't help hearing all these sounds, and it kept making her open her eyes and look toward the window. She thought she heard something again, then opened her eyes and thought she saw a shadow walk past her window. The shadow continued on, and she knew it was probably just someone walking on the sidewalk outside of her building, then she closed her eyes again.

Sleep, come on, wondrous sleep.

Finally, Mary dozed off, and soon she was snoring lightly. She didn't even hear the window being pulled open from the outside, nor did she hear it when a pair of very dirty shoes landed on her carpet. She did, however, hear her own name being whispered very close to her ear, and she opened her eyes with a gasp, just in time to feel the fingers as they tightened their grip around her neck.

Chapter 57

"FIRE!"

I had barely set foot inside the house before Alex jumped out in front of me, screaming the word. I grabbed my chest.

"Alex! You scared me!"

The boy swung his ax in the air, making noises like he was smashing a window, then ran off.

"Oh, good, you're home," Christine said as I entered the kitchen and put down my computer. She was eating cereal and handed me the empty milk jug. "We're out of milk. Again."

"Awesome," I said and threw the jug in the recycle bin.

"And we're out of clean underwear too. All of us."

I nodded and sat down on a stool next to her by the counter. "I see. And how was your day?"

She shrugged. "Normal."

"And school?"

She shrugged again and looked at her phone. "Usual."

I nodded, then looked at my watch. I could still make it to Publix before dinner and put in a load of laundry.

"Dad called today," she said like it was the most natural thing in the world. My eyes grew wide.

"Excuse me?"

"He called me. From Greece. Said he was coming home in two days. He wants to see us when he comes back. Can we go up there next weekend?"

"He wants to see you?" I asked, startled.

"That's what I just said," she said, annoyed.

"Well, I just..." I stopped myself. I couldn't really tell her that I had thought he didn't want to see them, but that was silly. I could see that now. Of course, he wanted to see them on weekends and vacations from time to time. He was, after all, their father. They had once been his entire life. What he didn't want anymore was the workload, all the trouble it was to take care of them.

"So, can we go?"

"Sure," I said.

She smiled. "Good. I can't wait to see him and hear about his trip. You think he bought us something?"

I nodded. "I'm sure he did."

She smiled again. "He better."

Christine finished her cereal, then left the kitchen, still playing some game on her phone. I chuckled, then decided to make the trip to Publix when my phone rang. It was from Alex's school. That was never a good sign. I picked it up.

"Eva Rae Thomas."

It was Alex's teacher, Miss Melanie. She sounded serious, and I braced myself for what Alex had gotten himself into now.

"We need to talk," she said. "Can you come in tomorrow? Say, around eleven o'clock?"

I swallowed and felt my hands go clammy. I knew Alex wasn't easy and wondered what he had been up to now.

"Sure," I said. "May I ask what this is about?"

"I prefer we talk about it when you come. See you tomorrow."

I put the phone down, feeling like I had just been called to the principal's office. I sighed, then walked up to Christine and told her to look after her baby brother while I went to Publix. On my way out the door, I texted Olivia and asked her what she was doing, why she hadn't come home from school yet, then received the answer that she had volleyball practice and that I really should know these things by now.

Chapter 58

MADDIE STARED at the letters scratched into the wall.

Sydney.

She couldn't stop wondering about this girl and who she was. Where was she now? Had she gone home to her mom? Was she back with her friends, back in school again, and was everything back to normal again? Maddie would give anything for normal right now. She would love to be able to go to school again, even to be faced with Gareth and his bullies. Even they would be better than what she was facing now.

The person inside the box had grown quiet, and there hadn't been a sound coming from in there all day. She wondered if this person was still in there at all. She had scratched on the outside of the box several times, but there had been no response. It felt devastating to Maddie because she felt like she had just found this person, she had just realized she wasn't alone in this, and yet now she somehow was again.

I miss my mommy. Why can't I just go home to her?

Maddie wondered if this was all her own fault. Maybe it was some sort of punishment? But for what? Could it be for breaking her mother's watch and not telling her about it? Could it be for the bad grades she had on her last report card and because she had signed it for her mommy because she didn't come home in time? And maybe because she didn't want her to see it because she'd only get mad at her because she wanted so badly for her to do better in life than she had?

Or was it because it was all her fault that her dad had left and that her mother had to work as a hooker? That's what Gareth and his friends had told her it was called. A dirty hooker. Did that mean Maddie was dirty too?

Maddie sniffled, then looked out under the blindfold, when suddenly there was a sound coming from outside the door. Maddie knew these sounds by now. The scrambling, the rustling, then the opening of locks, and soon the creaking of the door, followed by the heavy footsteps.

She knew the procedure by heart, and it always filled her with the greatest terror. Maddie gasped and realized she wouldn't be able to get back into her corner, so instead, she crumpled up into a ball by the opposite wall. The footsteps walking across the floor were determined, but they didn't come close to her. Instead, they walked to the box, then stopped. Out of the small crack under her blindfold, she could see a dolly being inserted underneath the box and it being lifted into the air, then rolled across the carpet toward the door. Maddie gasped as she saw it disappear out the door, then the door being slammed shut again behind it and the sound of it being locked.

Maddie sobbed when she realized that now she was actually all alone again. The person in the box was gone. She didn't know what this meant. Did the person get to go back to his or her family? Or was he...or she...?

Maddie didn't dare to finish the thought. Instead, she crumpled up on the floor next to the name on the wall, then cried till she exhausted herself so much that she fell asleep.

Chapter 59

I GRABBED three gallons of milk to make sure we could make it for a few days before I had to shop again, then got the rest of the items on my grocery list, and even added some candy for the kids. To sweeten their lives a little. I knew I was going to end up eating most of it, but I bought it anyway. Halloween was coming up at the end of the month, and you had to have sweets in your house.

I spotted him in aisle three. He was looking at cereal, holding a box of Cinnamon Toast Crunch out and putting it in his cart. I wondered who in his household ate that.

Phillip Anderson spotted me as I came closer and took two boxes of Cheerios.

"What? Are you stalking me now?" he asked. His nose looked swollen and crooked. It was still purple in places.

I looked into his cart. There was a roll of duct tape and zip tie strips. "To put up Halloween decorations," he said.

"I'm just getting cereal for my kids," I said.

"You're lucky I don't press charges; do you know that?" he asked.

"Well, I could say the same about you. How did you

convince her not to, huh? Did you tell her you'd beat her even more?"

Phillip looked at me, his teeth gritted. "I wasn't even with her when it happened."

I wrinkled my forehead. "You're lying!"

"You think you know me, huh?" he asked. "You've never even talked to me properly. You just come down here and start judging me. You have no idea who I am and what I am capable of."

"Wow. That sounded almost like a threat," I said.

He growled. "Argh, it doesn't matter what I say to you. You'll just twist it anyway. Don't you get it? I didn't hurt Dawn. I love her. I don't understand what happened. Yesterday, we were dating and having a wonderful time, and then suddenly today I hear she's in the hospital and everyone thinks I put her there. I've tried to call her, but her mom keeps answering the phone, telling me to stay away from her. I am completely freaking out, and I have my daughter coming this weekend, and I was hoping they'd meet. What if she hears these stories too? About me beating Dawn up?"

I paused. "Well...didn't you?"

"No! That's what I've been trying to say all this time. Even my colleagues at the station won't believe me. Everyone in this stupid town thinks I beat her up."

"Wait...Why should I believe you?" I said.

He threw out his arms. "I wasn't even with her last night. She was going home for dinner with her parents. I had coffee with her at Juice N' Java at three o'clock and then she kissed me and told me we'd see each other tomorrow. She had promised her mom she'd take her dad for a walk. He's in a wheelchair, you know? They like to drive out to Lori Wilson Park, and she helps him get all the way down to the beach. He loves it there. He misses the ocean."

"He was an excellent surfer back in the day," I said, remembering Dawn's dad in the lineup. It was always spectacular to watch him do tricks on his longboard. I chewed on this new information while my eyes locked with Phillip's, wondering what the heck was going on. If Phillip hadn't put Dawn in the hospital, then who had?

I left Phillip in the aisle, then rushed to the checkout, holding the phone between my shoulder and my ear while calling Melissa.

Chapter 60

MELISSA TOLD me Dawn had been discharged from the hospital and that she was staying with her parents, so her mother could take care of her. I drove to their house and parked in the driveway, my heart racing in my chest. What was going on here? I kept wondering.

I grabbed a bag of Reese's Peanut Butter Cups and walked up to her door, then rang the doorbell. Her mother opened it.

"Eva Rae? What a nice surprise." She wiped her hands on a dishtowel, then opened the door for me to enter. "I put her in her old room."

"How is she?" I asked.

Her mother shook her head and looked down. "Not good."

"Can I go see her?"

"Yes, yes, of course. Go ahead. You know your way."

I did. It was strange how being there again brought back so many memories and emotions I had completely forgotten. Inside her parents' house, it was as if time had stood still. Even the smell was the same as it had been back then. The furniture was all in the same place.

I knocked lightly on Dawn's old door, then peeked inside.

"Hey there."

"Eva Rae!"

She sat up in the bed, but I could tell by her strained face that she was in pain.

"I brought you chocolates," I said and handed her the bag.

She smiled. I opened the pack and fed her one. She could barely get it inside her swollen lips and winced in pain from where they were cracked. As she opened her mouth, I could tell that two of her front teeth were chipped.

I stuffed my mouth with two pieces at the same time, trying to suppress my desire to burst into tears. Dawn chewed cautiously, but it seemed to be more pain than pleasure for her.

"You want another one?" I asked.

She shook her head, and I exhaled, then ate another chocolate. I had a knot in my stomach, and a big part of me just wanted to run out of there, but I had to have some answers. I had to know what was going on with her. Something wasn't right.

"I punched Phillip," I said and grabbed her hand in mine.

"No!" she said, her swollen eyes lingering on me.

"Yes," I said with a chuckle. "Hit him right on the nose. I was that mad at him for what he did to you."

She slumped her head, and her eyes looked away.

"Dawn?" I paused. I really didn't want to ask about this, but I had to. "It wasn't him, was it? He didn't do this to you, did he?"

Dawn lifted her head and glared at me from inside the small cracks between her swollen eyelids. I could tell she was contemplating what to say to me. I let her think it over.

"It was never any of them, was it?" I asked and held her hand tightly in mine. "All the times you ended up in the hospital. It was never your boyfriends."

Her eyes lingered on me still; her nostrils were flaring lightly. I could tell she was getting agitated, scared even.

I leaned closer and squeezed her hand tightly. "It's okay,

Dawn. You can tell me. I remember how your dad used to beat you when we were children. My guess is the abuse never stopped. Am I right? Is it still him?"

Dawn's nostrils flared violently now, and she shook her head.

"It's okay, Dawn," I said. "You can tell me everything."

Dawn shook her head fiercely now and was breathing heavily. Her eyes were staring at me and fear seemed to be spiraling through her.

"What's wrong?" I asked, then turned to look at what was behind me. I barely managed to duck before the crowbar whooshed through the air and hit me on the shoulder. I screamed and fell to the floor, then looked up at Dawn's mother, who was hovering above me.

"This is my daughter," she almost screamed at me. "You're not going to take my daughter away from me, do you hear me?"

She swung the crowbar again, and it whistled through the air, then hit my arm. I screamed in pain.

"MOM, NO!"

Dawn screamed from behind me as her mother jammed the crowbar down on me once again, barely missing me as I rolled to the side. As I did, I reached down my leg and found my weapon and pulled it out of the ankle holster, then pointed it at her.

"Stop, Vivian," I panted. "It's over."

The woman's wild eyes glared down at me, and I could tell she didn't care. She swung the crowbar once again, and I fired my gun, hitting her in the shoulder. The shock was so great that she dropped the crowbar, then fell backward and landed against the dresser, her eyes struck with deep fear. I rose to my feet, still pointing the gun at her as she sank to the floor, blood gushing out of her wound.

Chapter 61

"SO, it was her the entire time?"

Melissa handed me a bottle of water, and I drank greedily, wishing it was something a little stronger. I was sitting with Dawn, who was still crying heavily. I couldn't get her to stop. I had given my statement to the police, and Dawn's mother had been taken away in an ambulance. The paramedics had also tended to my bruises. They wanted me to go in for an x-ray to see if anything was broken, but I told them I had to go home. I felt okay. I was sore and in pain, but I didn't think anything was broken.

Dawn nodded and looked up at Melissa. "I am so sorry, you guys. I should have...I should have told you. I lied to you."

"I can't believe it," Melissa said.

I nodded. "Me either. All those years, we believed it was your father who had beaten you up and...you were just covering for your mother?"

Dawn looked away. Tears spilled onto her bedcovers, and she wiped them away.

"Over the years, it got worse," she said. "And as I grew

older, I began saying it was my boyfriends. I didn't mean to lie or get them in trouble. It was just easier that way."

"And because it was too embarrassing to tell anyone that your mother still beat you," Melissa said.

"Using a crowbar, apparently," I said, feeling my sore shoulder.

"I...I tried to get away from her. I tried to stop visiting, but she was just...she had such a stronghold on me. It was like I was powerless. I don't know how she did it, but she always made me come back. She would guilt trip me or tell me my dad was sick, and then when I came to see him, she beat me. It was actually better if I came often because then she wouldn't touch me for a long time unless I upset her somehow. It was worst when I had boyfriends. She got so jealous and would tell me I was worthless, that he would leave me, that no one would ever marry me. I tried to hide them from her, but somehow, she always found out. A neighbor would tell her that she saw me with someone downtown or she would follow me in her car and see us together. And then she would become this monster, yelling at me that I wanted to leave her, that I was a loser and that I was destroying the family and making my dad upset. It was actually mostly to see him that I ever came home. I felt like I needed to be there for him. He was the one who was really trapped here with her."

"Wait...she put him in the wheelchair?" I asked.

Dawn nodded. "He was about to leave her. After so many years of abuse, he was a broken man, and then one day, he finally found the courage to stand up to her. She pushed him down the stairs, and he landed in the wrong way, getting paralyzed from the waist down."

"That way, she made sure he never could leave her, that he was forever dependent on her. Just like she made sure you were," I said. "If you never had a boyfriend, you'd never leave her. So, she destroyed every relationship you ever had. It was a way for her to control you."

"I still…I can't…It's sick. I can't believe I never saw this," Melissa said. "I just thought…I always thought you found these bad guys. I had no idea what you were going through, Dawn. I feel terrible. Poor you."

"It wasn't your fault," Dawn said, smiling between tears.

I couldn't hold mine back anymore either and, a few seconds later, we all three joined in a hug until Dawn groaned in pain and we had to let go of her.

"No more secrets," I said, wiping my tears away. "You hear me? The three of us, we need each other, and we can't be of help if we're not honest."

"Okay," Melissa said with a deep sniffle. "That's a deal."

"You start by telling us what's going on with Matt. And be honest," she said laughing.

I blew my nose, then threw the tissue at her.

"I do know one thing, though," I said. "I owe Phillip a major apology."

Dawn exhaled deeply. "So do I. If anyone owes him one, it must be me."

Chapter 62

I HAD CALLED my dad and asked him to be with the kids till I got back. It was late, and they were all asleep as I entered the house. Even my dad was napping on my couch in the living room, snoring loudly.

I woke him with a kiss on the forehead. He smiled happily. "You're back?"

I nodded and sat down with a deep sigh. He sat up and folded his hands. "That bad, huh?"

"Worse," I said. "I'll tell you about it another day. Right now, I am beat and just want to go to bed. Thanks for coming over."

"I'm glad I could be of help. Your mom has been out all day anyway."

"Where has she been?" I asked and put my feet up on the coffee table that my mom had bought for me because she said I couldn't have a house without a coffee table. I knew she would have a heart attack if she saw me put my dirty shoes on her expensive table, but I didn't care.

"Winter Park, visiting her girlfriends. They all live there now," he said. "Because of the gated communities and golf courses. And less risk of hurricane damage, they believe."

"Let me guess...she wants to go live there as well?" I asked.

"Well, naturally. The neighborhoods are far more well-trimmed, as she puts it."

"But you don't want that," I said.

"No. Of course not. I like it out here. I like the ocean breeze, and I like the surfers and the laid-back attitude. In there it's so...uptight. It's not for me. I need the ocean close. Makes it less unbearable in the summer too. I wouldn't last a day in there in the summer. Besides, I still have my business to attend to."

"You could do that in there," I said grinning, knowing that had probably been my mom's argument too.

"True. That's a lousy argument. But I am not going. End of discussion. If she wants to go see her friends in Winter Park, then she can do the drive."

"Sounds like something you guys can argue about for the next several years," I said.

My dad chuckled and got up. He leaned over and kissed my forehead. I pulled him into a hug, thinking about Dawn and all that she had been through. He put his arms around me. I closed my eyes and enjoyed being held.

"Don't give in to her," I said as he let go of me. "Ever."

He shook his head. "I won't."

I walked him out and then closed the door behind him, thinking I had been lucky with my parents after all. At least compared to Dawn. My mother was just coldhearted toward me. She had, after all, never laid a hand on me. I turned off the lights in the living room, then noticed something on the light carpet. I knelt and sighed, realizing it was some of Alex's green slime. It was deep into the carpet, and someone had stepped in it. It had left big marks all over the carpet and into the hallway. It was going to take forever to get out.

I sighed and decided that would have to wait till the morning, then walked up the stairs, and checked on the kids in their rooms before turning in. As soon as my head hit the pillow, I was sound asleep.

Chapter 63

"MOMMY. MOMMY! I GOT AN AWARD."

I am running through the house, holding the medal in my hand. The house is so quiet. It has been for months, ever since that day in Wal-Mart when Sydney was taken. It is fall now, four months into Kindergarten. I feel proud of myself.

"Look," I say and run into the kitchen, throwing my backpack on the floor as I go. My mom is standing in there, looking out into the backyard and the canal.

"Mom?" I say hoping to get her attention. "Look! I did the project all by myself."

She doesn't turn to look at me.

"What's wrong?" I say.

My mother shakes her head, then looks down at the potatoes she is peeling. "I was thinking maybe we should grow some petunias out in the yard, huh? I bet that would look nice."

"Sure, Mom, but...I won an award. In school?"

My mother doesn't look at me. She shakes her head while peeling the potatoes. "Pick up your backpack from the floor. It doesn't go there. If you keep throwing it there, someone will trip over it."

"But...Mom?"

"Now," she says.

I stare at her back, thinking I can't remember when I saw her eyes the last time, or when I felt her kiss.

"Sydney has a doll in her room, the American girl doll, can I go play with it?" I ask.

It's the first time I've mentioned her name since that day. I haven't dared to, but I really love that doll. And now it's just in there gathering dust like all her other stuff. Every day, I walk to the door and open it, then look inside, but I never dare to go in there. A doll should be played with and not just sit there.

My mother's back turns curvy as she takes in a deep breath. The response comes promptly.

"NO!"

"But, Mo-om, that doll is brand new, and no one is playing with it."

My mom no longer pays me any attention. She shuts up like a clam and doesn't say a word to me, no matter how much I beg. She just freezes me out and, finally, I give up. I turn around and walk out of the kitchen, picking up my backpack on the way. My mom doesn't speak to me for three days after this, and after that, only with short words without even looking at me. I tug at her dress, I yell her name as loud as I can, but she simply ignores me.

I sat up in bed and let the tears crawl down my cheeks. My pillow was soaked from me crying in my sleep. I felt so overwhelmed inside; I couldn't stop crying. For years, I had forgotten how my mother had shut me out back then. I knew she had, but I had forgotten how lonely it had made me, how inadequate it had made me feel. I guess I needed to put all that somewhere in the back of my mind in order to move on, in order to make it in life. But now that I was back in Cocoa Beach, it was like it had decided to pour out and completely overpower me. There was nothing I could do.

I went to the bathroom and found a box of tissues, then wiped my nose, remembering how I used to get on my knees in my old room and pray to God to allow me to go back in time so the kidnapper could take me instead of her, crying to him, asking him why it had to be me? Why did I have to survive?

It still made no sense to me.

Sensing how thirsty I was, I walked down the stairs into the kitchen and turned on the light. It was still very dark outside, and the clock showed only midnight. I hadn't been asleep for very long. I wondered if I was going to get any more sleep. The emotions from the dream still lingered with me and made me want to cry more.

I grabbed a glass from the cabinet when I spotted a figure outside my window, and I dropped it.

Chapter 64

"MATT? WHAT THE HECK?"

He pointed at the front door, and I ran to open it.

"What are you doing out there scaring me half to death?"

The look in his eyes startled me, and I knew he wasn't joking around. Something was wrong.

"I came to see you," he said. "Then I spotted you in the window and thought, if I could get your attention, we wouldn't have to wake up the kids. Something's happened. Can I come in?"

"Of course," I said and stepped aside to let him in. He rushed to my kitchen and put down his laptop.

"Matt, you look awful," I said. "Can I get you something? A glass of water?"

He looked at me. "Do you have something stronger?"

"Wine? Whiskey?"

He nodded. "A scotch please."

"That bad, huh?" I asked and poured him a glass. I handed it to him, and he downed it in one gulp. Matt had never been much of a drinker, so I was very surprised to see this. A little frightened too, to be honest.

"Worse," he said and put the glass down with a grimace.

The alcohol seemed to give him color back in his cheeks, but only for a few seconds. He opened the laptop and tapped on the keyboard. I walked up behind him, clutching my glass of water in my hand, bracing myself for something terrible.

"What is it, Matt?" I asked. "A new video?"

He nodded. "Yes. I was about to go to bed when I received it. It was sent to me directly. Just like last time. I'm beginning to think this guy has something against me personally."

"Or maybe it's just because he knows you're on the case. You have been on the news quite a few times talking about Sophie Williams' disappearance and the finding of her body. He might just have picked you because of that."

"Okay, but how do you explain this then?" he said and opened a video, then started it. I sat on a stool next to him and watched it with him. It showed a box made from wood. On the side of it, someone had painted the word ALONE.

Next, text appeared on the screen.

Loneliness. Divorce often leads to a profound sense of loneliness for the children involved. As parents move into new homes and custodial parents get caught up in trying to make it through each day, children are often left feeling lonely and all alone. This child will often demand unusual amounts of attention from his or her parents. He or she might smile constantly and try to keep everyone happy, hoping to keep peace between the parents. Others might withdraw from friends and family or express anger in order to get attention. Some turn to goofing around or getting in fights to gain attention. Common to all of these is a feeling of isolation from the world.

The text stopped, and the video clipped to another picture, taken from inside the box. A young child was sitting inside of it, bent over like he was sleeping. The video sped up, and we could see him wake up, then start knocking on the sides of the box, hammering it, crying helplessly. As the video progressed, the child became more and more apathetic, and the hammering turned to knocking and a strained face as he called out. The knocking soon became scratching till the boy barely moved anymore.

Then, Matt stopped it.

"What...what the hell is this, Matt?"

"A boy, isolated from the world, slowly dying from his loneliness, is my guess." He rubbed his forehead. "If you look at the date in the corner, you'll see that this has been recorded over a long period of time. Two months, it looks like."

"Has that boy been in that box for two whole months?" I said. "He must have fed him then."

Matt nodded, biting his nails. I had never seen him do that before. That was new.

"Matt?"

"There's more," he said.

"Okay?"

"The boy. He's...he's my son."

Chapter 65

IT TOOK me a few seconds before the realization slowly sunk in. I kept staring at Matt while the thoughts fluttered in my mind.

"You have a son?"

Matt nodded, still biting his nails. "Elijah. He's eight."

"How...you never mentioned him?"

Matt's eyes were avoiding mine. I saw hurt in them. "I don't see him much. His mom has custody of him. It was all a mess. He was an accident—a one-night-stand. I was never really a part of his life. The last few years, she hasn't been letting me see him much."

"When did you see him last?" I asked.

"In April."

"But that was six months ago?"

Matt rubbed his forehead. "I know. I checked the database; she hasn't reported him missing."

I wrinkled my forehead. "That's odd. Have you called her?"

He nodded. "It was the first thing I did. She doesn't answer."

I looked at the clock on my stove. It was past midnight. I grabbed my phone and put it in my pocket.

"I'll drive."

I woke up Olivia and told her she was in charge for a few hours while I took care of some work. She blinked a few times, then sighed.

"I thought you stopped all that."

"Yeah, you and me both, baby. But this is urgent."

Olivia gave me a look to let me know she understood it was important. Matt and I took off and soon drove out of Cocoa Beach.

His ex lived in Vieira, a town on the mainland about twenty-five minutes from my house. It was one of those newer neighborhoods that had shot up in the past few years. There was a big water fountain at the entrance, and the bushes and trees were nicely trimmed, and everything was clean and pretty, but all the houses looked exactly alike. Just like had they been cut out with the same cookie cutter. To me, it all came out as bland, and I knew I would suffocate if I lived in a neighborhood like this. That's what I liked about Cocoa Beach. No two houses were the same. It was messy and a little rough in places, but it had charm.

We parked the car outside in the well-trimmed driveway and walked up the lawn. I noticed that Matt's hand was shaking as he rang the doorbell. I sent him a comforting smile, but it didn't help.

No one opened the door, and he rang again. When nothing happened still, he opened the screen door and started hammering on the wooden door behind it. He was going to wake up the entire neighborhood, but I had a feeling he didn't care about that right now.

"POLICE. OPEN UP!"

A light was turned on in the house next door. I saw the blinds being pulled aside. There was going to be a lot of talking once morning came. No doubt about that.

It concerned me that no one still opened the door after Matt had been yelling. Since it woke up the neighbors, it had to wake up the woman inside this house too.

"Lisa?" he yelled. "I need to talk to you. Now," Matt yelled.

I gave him a look. "Could she be somewhere else?"

He shook his head. "She doesn't have family around here."

"Friends?"

He swallowed. "Sure. She has a few."

I walked to a window and peeked inside, placing my face close to the glass. I couldn't escape the feeling that something was very much off here. Why hadn't the woman put out a missing person's report for her child? If he really had been in that box for two months, she'd had plenty of time to figure out he was gone. Unless the person making the video was just messing with us, and he hadn't been gone that long after all. Except this guy didn't seem to be messing around at all. Everything else he had done had been very seriously and very well planned out. He hadn't taken any shortcuts and had been planning this in very small detail for months, maybe even years. And so far, all we had been able to do was to play by his rules. It was time to change that up; it was time for us to get ahead, but how? So far, his next move had been impossible to figure out in advance. They had all come as surprise attacks.

"I see something," I said, then looked at Matt, concern in my eyes. My heart started pounding. "I see legs poking out from behind a couch. We need to get inside. Asap."

Chapter 66

I DIDN'T HAVE to say that twice to Matt. He kicked the door open, and we both went into the hallway, holding our weapons out in front of us. The sweet yet nauseating stench that met us made me feel sick to my stomach. I knew that smell a little too well...the sulfurous gas that a putrefying body gives off after having been dead for some time. It was similar to the smell of rotten eggs. I covered my mouth and nose with my sleeve. Matt did the same, gagging as he went along.

"Police!"

"It was in the living room," I said.

Matt entered to the right to clear the kitchen, then came back out and nodded.

"Clear."

We continued into the living room, scanning the room first, making sure no one was hiding in there. And that was when we saw her—a woman lying on the carpet by the couch. I turned on the light, and we walked to her. Matt gasped and clasped his mouth, then knelt next to her.

"Lisa," he whispered.

"Looks like blunt force trauma to the back of her head," I

said and pointed at the pool of dried up blood surrounding her head like a halo. Flies and maggots crawled in her ears and eye sockets. Her eyes had been pushed out of their sockets, and her tongue was forced out of her mouth. That was also due to the gas and bloating buildup inside the body as it was decomposing. All the fluids and gas had leaked out of her body; her skin had ruptured and fallen off her bones.

"Nails and hair have fallen out," I said. "Which tells us she's been here for more than a month. My guess is that the decay has been slowed down by the fact that she's been lying inside air-conditioning. A good guess will be that she was killed on the day someone took Elijah, two months ago, but of course, we'll need the medical examiner's report to verify that."

Matt stared at her dead body, shaking his head, eyes wet. "Oh, dear God, Lisa. No."

"I am so sorry, Matt," I said. "I'll call it in."

With the phone against my ear, I walked outside to get out of the stench and be able to talk. A few neighbors had gathered outside their houses now to see what was going on. A couple from across the street was staring at me, holding onto one another, their faces struck with fear. As I hung up, I walked to them, trying to look reassuring.

"What's going on?" the woman asked, her voice shaking.

"Police investigation," I said.

"Did something happen to Lisa?" the woman asked, breathing in small gasps.

"I am afraid so, and I would like to ask you a few questions; can I do that?"

The husband looked briefly at his wife, then nodded. "Of course."

"Have you seen anything suspicious around here, anything out of the ordinary around Lisa's house? A car maybe? People hanging out there whom you haven't seen before?"

They exchanged a look briefly, then looked back at me. "No, not that we can think of," the wife answered. "We did talk the other day about how long ago it was that we had seen the little boy. We used to always see him riding his bike around in the cul-de-sac. But we hadn't seen the mother either, so we just assumed they were out of town or maybe just busy, you know?"

"We did talk about if they might have moved," the husband added.

"You didn't notice a smell?" I asked.

They looked at one another again, then the wife gasped. "The smell? Oh, yes…what that…? Oh, dear Lord."

She clasped her mouth with a whimper. Her husband pulled her closer. "We did talk about a strange smell in the neighborhood a couple of weeks ago but assumed it came from somewhere else. Maybe the sewers or the lake. We could never imagine…it coming from over there?"

I nodded. "We believe the crime may have been committed two months ago…"

"Two months ago..?" the wife said with a shrill voice. "But… but…"

"I need you to try and think back. Two months ago, did anything unusual happen around here? Any cars drive by that you didn't know?" I asked. "Anyone walk up to the house that made you wonder who he or she was?"

The wife pondered while the husband shook his head. "That's a very long time ago. I don't think we…"

"Wait," she said and held a hand up to stop him. "We're talking back in August, right?"

"Yes?"

"That's when Daniel was there."

"Daniel who?" the husband asked.

"From the paper."

"I don't remember any Daniel from the paper," the husband said.

"Well, that's because you're never home; you're always out on that golf course." She looked at me, shaking her head. "Nevertheless, there was this guy, this reporter, from *Florida Today* who wanted to do a story about Elijah," she continued. "Because he was such a great baseball talent. He followed him for a couple of days around for practice and so on. Come to think of it, I never read the story in the paper…"

"Okay," I said and wrote it down on my notepad. "This is very good. So, there was a reporter there; Daniel, you say his name was?"

The woman nodded. "Yes."

"Do you know his last name?"

She shook her head. "I'm afraid not."

"Do you remember anything else about him? What did he look like?" I asked.

"Well, he was tall. Taller than Fred," she said and glanced at her husband. "And he's six foot two, so I'll say about six foot four or so."

I wrote it down. "Okay, good, anything else? Color of hair and eyes? Any special birthmarks or facial hair?"

"Brown hair, brown eyes, and a mustache. Kind of reminded me of Burt Reynolds. I used to love that guy. Too bad he passed. The mustache wasn't as thick as Burt's, though."

"Did he drive a car?"

"Oh, yes, a blue BMW convertible. Flashy little thing." She paused pensively. "Are you trying to locate him? I'm sure if you call the newspaper, they'll help you find him."

Fred sighed and rolled his eyes. "Don't you understand? He was never from the newspaper. That's why the article was never printed."

His wife looked at him, annoyed. "I know that."

"Well, we don't know about that yet, but thank you so much for your help. I'll probably be back for more information later. Did he say anything about where he lived?"

"I never really spoke to him myself," she said. "It was mostly what Lisa told me."

"Okay. Was there anything else, anything that stood out to you about him?"

The small woman sighed, then shook her head. "He seemed like such a nice guy."

I nodded. "They all do, ma'am."

Chapter 67

I STAYED at the crime scene all night while the techs searched Lisa's house. We had explained the situation to them and asked them to secure anything that might give us a clue as to where her son might be.

At five o'clock, we drove back toward Cocoa Beach. I had kids I needed to wake up and get ready for school. I told Matt he could come back to my house and crash on my couch for a little while. I figured it was a bad idea for him to be alone right now.

"You need the rest. If you want to find your son, you need to sleep first," I said when he started to argue.

My kids were exhausted and, somehow, they all three managed to get themselves in a fight during breakfast. But, for once, I managed to get Alex to the bus on time, and both girls rode their bikes to school. It was a small victory, but at this point, I took what I could get. I made some coffee then went to the living room where I thought Matt was sleeping. But, of course, he wasn't. How could he? I knew I wouldn't be able to. Instead, he was sitting with his laptop on his knees, watching the video over and over again.

I handed him a cup of coffee, and he took it.

"Do you think he's still alive?" he asked, staring at the screen, where he had stopped the video of Elijah curled up inside of the box, not moving.

I fought my desire to cry when thinking of that poor boy trapped inside that awful box, then sat down with my coffee between my hands. Images of Lisa's decomposed body rushed across my mind as I briefly closed my eyes.

"All we can do is hope," I said.

"It seems like such a fragile thing to cling to, doesn't it?" Matt said. "Hope. If this guy wants him dead, then he's probably dead, right?"

"We don't know that."

"I spoke to IT," he said, sipping his coffee. "They're trying to trace it. Both emails were sent from a newly created account using Proton Mail, a secure email based in Switzerland. The named used is fake and so is all the other information."

"And the IP address?" I asked.

"Led us to a Starbucks on 520. According to our IT guys, it is most likely that our guy bought a cheap tablet with cash, took that tablet to the local Starbucks, then logged onto their free Wi-Fi, uploaded the video to YouTube, sent the email, then destroyed the tablet afterward."

"And the tablet couldn't somehow be traced?" I asked.

"Some models do send model numbers or even serial numbers, but even if they were able to identify where it was bought, this guy probably bought it with cash, and that means there's no tracing him. At least that's what they told me last time."

I growled and clenched my fist in anger. This guy was just always one step ahead of us. It annoyed me immensely. It was almost as if he knew as much about how the police worked as we did.

"Could he be an inside guy?" I asked cautiously. This type of accusation wasn't something you'd just throw around lightly in the force.

Matt bit his lip and our eyes locked for a few seconds. I shook my head. "Nah, you can probably find all this information online. There are DIY tutorials for everything these days. I saw one recently for how to break into a hotel room. Nice."

I took another sip of my coffee while staring at Matt's screen. Matt placed a finger on Elijah's face. It was torture to watch. I finished my cup, then put it down. I looked at Matt again.

"Say, aren't we missing something?"

"What do you mean?"

"The killer put the others, Sophie, Scott, and Nathaniel, on display for us to find, right? Why haven't we found Elijah yet? Nathaniel Pullman was also in a video, and we were supposed to find him. The killer knew we would, that's why he chose the place that he did."

"So...you're saying we should be looking for a clue of where to find him?"

I nodded. "Let's watch the video again."

Matt played it again. About halfway through, something happened. There was a brief clip in the footage, and I asked Matt to pause it.

"Look."

"What am I looking at?"

"Can you go like one frame back?"

"I can try," he said, then pulled the cursor backward just enough for a picture to show up.

"The video was fast-forwarded to show us the time Elijah spent in there. In the middle, he inserted a picture that we wouldn't see if we didn't slow it down. See?"

Matt looked at me, then nodded. "But what is it?"

"It's a picture of a sign," I said.

"I can see that, but what does it mean?"

"It's from the port."

"But...but the port is a pretty big place?" he said.

I nodded, then rose to my feet. "Call Chief Annie on our way there. We might need a couple of your colleagues to help us."

Chapter 68

IT WAS STILL DARK out when Maddie opened her eyes. With the little light that was left in the room, she could see that the box was still gone.

She was alone.

Maddie sighed and kicked her legs to be able to turn herself around and look out underneath the blindfold. As she stared in the direction of where the box had been, she spotted something on the floor. Not knowing what it was, she wormed herself closer, then looked at it up close.

A nail.

A nail that had to have fallen out of the box when it was moved. Maddie couldn't believe it. She stared at the small thing, excitement—mixed with a load of fear—emerging in her stomach. Was this her break? Was this her chance?

She used her legs to turn her back to the nail, then moved her fingers to see if she could grab it. Her wrists throbbed painfully from behind the zip tie strips, but still, she managed to get the nail up between her fingers. Happily, she grunted in excitement, but then dropped the nail again. Maddie cursed herself for being clumsy, then felt her way to it again, found it, and once again picked it up between her thumb and pointer finger. Straining in concentration, she now fiddled with it till she got the pointy end placed at the lock of the strip. Using her pointer finger, she pushed it hard against the lock, but it slipped and poked her wrist instead. Sobbing in pain, she dropped the nail again.

Come on, Maddie. Stop being so freakin clumsy! This is your only chance.

Maddie took in another deep breath, then felt her way to the nail once more, grabbed it, and placed it back against the lock, pushed it down, forcefully, and felt how it pierced the plastic. The nail was now stuck in the lock and, with much force, Maddie wiggled it around, and suddenly the strip snapped.

Maddie laughed, a little startled, then pulled her hands up in front of her face and pulled off the blindfold completely. She grabbed the nail, then poked it through the plastic strip tying her feet together. Seconds later, she could move her legs again. Exhausted from the lack of food and drink, she now regained much of her strength just at the mere prospect of getting free and maybe escaping.

Mom, I am coming home.

Maddie rose to her feet, got dizzy from standing up too fast, and had to lean against the wall so she wouldn't fall. Her legs were wobbly, but she walked the few steps toward the window, where she peeked out through the crack in the shutters. Then she gasped. She was higher up than she had expected. She looked at the door, then ran to it and pulled the handle, but as she had expected, it was locked. Maddie returned to the window again. She grabbed the small tab poking out on top and unlocked it, then pulled it open. She couldn't believe the relief she felt when breathing in the fresh air once again. She put her nose close to the screen to take it all in.

She looked down through the cracks. Below her was a yard and a screened pool area. She was in someone's house.

Thinking she heard a sound coming from outside the door, she gasped once again and turned to look. There was a rustling behind it.

Her perpetrator was coming back, and there was no one else in the room other than her. Her captor had to be coming to kill her.

As the door was unlocked, Maddie stared through the crack at what was down below her. The yard ended in a seawall and the canal where all the boats passed by. Those had to be the engines Maddie had heard from time to time.

More rustling behind the door and now the handle was turning.

You've got to do something, Maddie. Now!

As the door opened and Maddie once again locked eyes with her captor, she did something she would never have thought possible.

She kicked her foot through the screen, then kicked the hurricane shutters as hard as she could, again and again, till they got loose and fell out, then pushed her body out the window, through the hole in the screen, and slid down the side of the roof till she reached the end of it and managed to stop when grabbing on to a tile on the roof. Then, as her captor yelled behind her and came to the window, she didn't even look back.

She stood up, ran as fast as she could toward the edge of the roof, closed her eyes, and jumped.

Chapter 69
THEN

SHE CAME to them one day as they were walking home from the school bus. She was waiting in the car at the bus stop and, as they began to walk, she drove after them, then rolled down the window.

"Hi there, sweetie."

The boy refused to look at her, but his sister couldn't hide her enthusiasm. The boy knew it was harder for her to understand how wicked their mother really was and how important it was for them to stay as far away from her as possible. But he did. The boy knew more than her, and it was his job to protect her. He understood what his dad told them and had taken it all to heart. He knew that it didn't matter how sweet she talked or how much she pleaded. It was important to keep her away and not give in to the emotions they might feel. 'Cause that was her trick. That was the way she would try and manipulate them. The boy wasn't quite sure he understood what exactly manipulate meant, but he knew it was bad.

"Hi, Momma!"

The boy shushed his sister, then pulled her arm forcefully to get her to walk a little faster. They weren't that far from their house, and in there, they would be safe. There was no telling what their mother might be on right now.

"Come on," he hissed at her, but his sister didn't want to walk anymore. She stopped and looked at her mommy in the car. She pulled her arm out of his grip, then walked to the open window and peeked inside.

"Hi there, baby. How was school?" their mother said.

"Great," the girl said. "I made a turkey."

His baby sister lifted the turkey that she had made by tracing her hands and feet. The boy rolled his eyes, then rushed to her and pulled her shoulder.

"We have to go. Now."

"No," his sister said.

And that was when the boy accidentally lifted his eyes and looked into those of his mother. And that was when he was betrayed. His emotions did it to him; they overwhelmed him and brought tears to his eyes.

"Hi, baby. How are you?" his mommy said.

The boy stared at her, then swallowed.

"We have to go; come on," he said addressed to his sister.

"I don't want to," his sister said angrily.

"Mom and Dad would be so angry if they knew what we were doing," he said.

"Mom, huh?" his mommy said. "You call her that?"

"She's our new mom," he answered.

The hurt in his mother's eyes was painful to watch, and he looked away. She exhaled.

"How about I take you two out for some ice cream, huh? What do you say?"

"Yay!" his baby sister exclaimed.

The boy shook his head. "We can't. We have to go home, come."

But his sister wouldn't hear of it. She grabbed the door handle, pulled the door open, and jumped inside the car before the boy could stop her. She giggled and strapped herself down, then yelled at him to come too.

"Just for half an hour," his mommy said and held out her hand toward him. "They'll never know. Come."

"Yes, come on!" his baby sister squealed from the back seat. "Don't be a party pooper."

The boy threw a brief glance down the road toward their house, then grabbed his mother's hand and jumped inside too.

Chapter 70

"HOW DO you know where to go?"

We had parked the car at the port, and I was rushing off, Matt running after me. Tall cruise ships towered in front of us, along with several enormous cargo ships.

"I had a good friend in elementary school. Her dad worked at the docks," I said and ran down a dock where a big cargo ship was being loaded.

"And?" Matt asked as I slowed down, searching for what I remembered. "We used to come down here and play. I remember how there used to be...over there," I said and pointed. We ran the last part under a big crane.

"What's his statement?" I asked. "What's he trying to say?"

"Loneliness?" Matt said. "That kids in a divorce are often lonely?

"Yes, but more than that. It's also that Elijah is one in a crowd, only one out of many."

"Yes...and?"

I stopped and looked in front of me. Matt did too. In front of us was what looked like several hundreds of wooden boxes exactly like the one we had seen in the video. Some of them were being loaded onto the ship in front of us.

"Oh, dear God," Matt said, panting. "How? How are we supposed to find him?"

"We're looking for one with the word ALONE painted on the side of it," I said and looked around anxiously for someone to ask. There was a guy in a forklift, transporting three boxes of the same type as ours onto the ship, then returning. I ran to him, then waved my hands.

"Hey!"

He stopped and looked out. "What?"

"Police," I said. "We're looking for a wooden box."

The man grinned a toothless grin. "I got plenty of those."

"It's got something written on the side. A word. ALONE. Have you seen it?" I asked, yelling through the noise from a huge cargo ship sailing past us, tooting their horn as they passed.

"Sure," he said. "I remember seeing it."

My eyes grew wide. "Great! Where?"

He nodded in the direction of the ship passing us. "I loaded it onto that one there. Earlier this morning."

My heart dropped as I saw the end of the big ship with the words SANTA MONICA on its back sail out of the canal.

Chapter 71

WATER SPLASHED in my face as we raced across the waves. Matt had gotten ahold of the coast guard, and they had taken us on board. The cargo ship had left the harbor completely and was far in the horizon as we rushed toward it, bumping along. Meanwhile, Matt was on the radio, trying to get ahold of the ship's captain to get them to slow down and let them know we were coming on board.

While we shot through the big ocean, my phone rang. It was from Alex's school. I picked it up, barely able to hear the person on the other end.

"Hello, Ms. Thomas? Melanie Lawson here."

Miss Melanie? Alex's teacher? *Oh, no, the meeting!* I had completely forgotten about the meeting I was called into. I looked at my watch. It was almost eleven thirty.

"I am so sorry, Mrs. Lawson, something came up."

"I figured as much," she said, sounding like she was personally offended that I hadn't shown up. I looked at Matt's concerned face as I spoke, reminding myself that right now this was more important. I couldn't allow myself to feel guilty over this. A boy's life was on the line.

"Could I come in later, maybe?" I asked.

I heard her sigh on the other end. "How about three o'clock?" she asked.

"Three o'clock sounds fantastic," I said, then hung up, secretly hoping I would be able to come in at three. There was no telling how long it would take to find that box.

We climbed onboard the ship, and they began opening the containers one after another. Three of Matt's colleagues were with us, among them Chris Cooper. I could tell Matt was out of it as I watched him frantically stare into one container after another. As I looked at how many containers there were on the ship, I realized this might take more than a few hours. This could take days.

"I found something!"

It was Chris. He called from the other end of the mountain range of containers. We rushed to him. He stood in front of an open container filled to the brim with wooden boxes.

"How do we do this?" Matt asked, rubbing his hair frantically. "It could be one of those, but it could also be in one of the other containers. How do we even check them? We have to turn the ship around. We need a forklift to get them out. We might have to go through all of them." The sound of deep despair was seeping through his voice. "And by the time we get to the right one, Elijah might be dead."

"I'll talk to the captain," Chris said and was about to leave when I heard something.

"Wait."

"What?" Matt asked.

I signaled for them all to remain silent, then walked closer to the stacked boxes. I put my ear to one of them when I heard it again.

"I hear something," I said. "It sounds like...a scraping!"

"It could be a rat," Chris said. "Plenty of them on ships like these."

Matt's face lit up. He disappeared for a second, and we

heard glass being broken, and he returned with a fire ax between his hands.

"Which one?"

"Matt," I said. "You can't do that. You risk hurting him if he's inside."

"Which one?" he said again. "Where did you hear the noise from?"

I swallowed. "Middle row...the one on the very end, but...Matt."

"Elijah, this is your father. If you can hear me, move away from the sides of the box. Move into the middle. I'm coming in!"

I tried to protest once again, but he wouldn't listen. Matt swung the ax at the bottom of the box, and it cracked. He swung it again, and this time it went through. He then reached up and peeked inside. I could hear him sobbing between agitated pants. He looked inside the box, then reached in and grabbed something.

A second later, he pulled a lifeless body out of the box by the legs. He grabbed him in his arms, then staggered toward us, his face torn in pain and anguish. I rushed to him and helped him put the boy down on the ground.

"Is he...?" he asked.

I felt for a pulse but found nothing.

"He must be alive, right?" Matt asked. "I mean, you heard him; you heard the scraping. He must have been alive then, right? That was just a few minutes ago...?"

He looked at me as if I held all the answers, while I frantically searched for the boy's pulse. I shook my head, then placed my hand on the boy's chest and pushed it down, then blew air into his lungs. I kept repeating this for a minute or so. It felt like an hour. Meanwhile, Matt sat on his knees. He cried and prayed for his boy to be alive. I blew one more time into his lungs, then I put my ear to his chest and heard a heartbeat.

"I got a heartbeat!" I yelled. "I've got a heartbeat!"

I stared at Matt, whose eyes lit up in the middle of the gloom.

"I did," I said. "I heard his heartbeat. I can feel it now. His pulse. He's alive, Matt. He's alive!"

Matt laughed and grabbed the boy in his arms, then held him up. He rocked him back and forth while repeating that he was going to be okay, over and over again.

Chris had the coast guard call for help, and soon a helicopter arrived, taking both Matt and Elijah with them. I looked after them as they were airlifted into the chopper, my heart jumping with joy.

We had won one. This time, the victory belonged to us.

Chapter 72

"MOMMY, WAKE UP. PLEASE?"

Rylan grabbed his mother's cold hand and pulled it. When that didn't help, he kissed her like they did in the story of *Snow White*. He had been reading it to his baby sister, Faith, over and over again for the past few days, not knowing what else to do. Their mommy had to have been very tired since she was still sleeping.

"I'm hungry," Faith whimpered and held her stomach.

Rylan was too. They had eaten all the crackers they had found in the cabinet on the first day. The box was empty, and now their stomachs were growling again. There was a box of Cheerios in there too, and now Rylan grabbed it and started to eat out of the box, then handed it to his sister. The milk in the fridge smelled bad, and they didn't want to drink it. There was some juice left, and he poured them each half a glass, then the jug was empty. Then they drank and ate while looking at their mother in her bed. They hadn't left her side since the first morning they had woken up and realized she hadn't.

"I'm still thirsty," his sister said as she emptied the juice glass.

"There's only water now," he said.

He grabbed a chair and pulled it close to the cabinets, then crawled up and found a new glass for her before pulling the chair to the fridge and crawling up on it, managing to fill the glass with water. He then slid down and handed his sister the glass that she drank from greedily. When she was done, she gave him one of those smiles that their mother loved so much.

"I miss Mommy," his sister said, almost crying again.

"Me too," Rylan said. "She will wake up soon. She was just really tired."

"Do you think she's sick?" Faith asked, standing in the doorway to the bedroom, looking at their mother.

Rylan shook his head. "She's not warm. She doesn't have a fever. She's very cold."

Faith wrinkled her nose. "She smells funny."

Rylan nodded. He had noticed it too. And the night before when he had crept into her bed and laid close to her, he hadn't been able to hear her heartbeat like he usually did. And she hadn't put her arm around him as she usually did. And this morning, the smell was worse than the day before, and he had to hold his nose when he went to check on her and see if she had finally woken up.

"Mommy needs to take a shower," Faith said and grimaced.

"She will," Rylan said. "As soon as she wakes up. She's just really tired; that's all."

"But she needs to take care of us," Faith complained, the sides of her mouth turning downward. Rylan hated when her mouth did that and rushed to hug her.

"Shh," he said like Mommy used to. He also stroked her hair the same way she used to do it and spoke the same words he believed she would have said:

"Don't worry. I'll take care of you until she wakes up. Don't worry, baby girl."

Faith sobbed a few times, then stopped. Rylan felt awkward trying to act like Mommy. He really wished she would hurry up and wake up soon because he was running out of hugs and nice words to say.

Chapter 73

"YOUR SON HAS BEEN QUITE disruptive in class."

Miss Melanie looked up from her papers. I sunk into the seat, feeling like a child at the principal's office. It was a quarter past three before I made it there, and me being late didn't impress Miss Melanie much. I had been late because I was on the phone with Matt, who called me from the hospital to let me know that Elijah was awake. He was severely dehydrated, and as soon as they got his levels back up, he opened his eyes and looked at Matt, then told him he was hungry for spaghetti and meatballs. He couldn't walk, though, since his legs were still too weak from not being used for two months.

"I've seen the notes," I said. "The ones you have him bring home."

She folded her hands in front of her. "We can't have this type of behavior in class. It's unfair to the other students."

"Listen," I said. "His dad and I are going through a divorce. He hasn't seen his father for several weeks now since his dad has been…well, busy. I know that the divorce must be taking a toll on him, with all the changes and the moving and all. I'm sure that, as soon as it all settles down and we get into a good rhythm, then he will calm down too."

Miss Melanie nodded. "I am aware of your situation, and I know these things can be very traumatizing for a young child, but I still think there is more to it than just that. I believe he is a child that needs a little extra attention, and I suggest we have him tested for…"

Oh, no. Here it comes. She wants him tested for ADHD.

"I am sorry," I interrupted her. "I don't think that's necessary. If we only give him a little time to settle down, I'm sure he will get better. Just give him a little time."

Miss Melanie cleared her throat. "Ms. Thomas, I really think he could benefit from being tested…"

"But I don't. These kids, once they get a diagnosis like that, it will follow them for the rest of their lives. It'll be in all his records, and he'll be stigmatized. I don't believe in labels. And then they'll want to medicate him. I don't want my child to be popping pills at this age. I don't think it's necessary and I believe too many children run around with a diagnosis on them when all they need is a little attention or help to get through a tough situation. I don't think my son has ADHD; I just think he's going through a rough patch right now, as are we all."

Miss Melanie looked at me in a questioning manner. She shook her head lightly.

"Who mentioned anything about ADHD?"

I gaped. "Uh…you did?"

She chuckled. "I most certainly did not. I was asking for your permission to have him tested for our gifted program. We believe your son is very smart and that he isn't getting the challenge he needs in school. We often see kids act out and become very vocal under these circumstances. I think your son could benefit tremendously from our program. With your permission, I'll have him tested, and he can join as soon as possible."

I stared at the woman in front of me, wishing for a small space I could crawl into. Me and my big mouth.

"So…do I have it? Your permission?" she asked.
I nodded, biting my tongue. "Where do I sign?"

Chapter 74

I HAD BARELY ENTERED the house before I could hear the kids screaming and yelling at one another. Alex was shooting his toy police gun at Christine, while she was eating a sandwich, and Christine was yelling at him to stop.

"Hi, guys," I said and entered the kitchen.

"Mommy!" Alex yelled, then threw himself in my arms. I hugged him tightly, reminding myself how fortunate I was that it wasn't my kid that had spent two months locked up in some box. I held him for a little longer than he cared for and, as soon as I let go of him, he stormed into the living room.

Christine was on her phone, grumbling something.

"What's with you?" I asked.

She sighed, then grumbled again. I couldn't hear what she said. I walked to the coffee maker and made a fresh pot. Two nights with barely any sleep made it hard to keep it together. It was going to require a lot of coffee to make it through the day.

"So, I've been thinking," I said. "About next week. How about you take Friday off and then go early to see your dad? Make it a long weekend? I haven't talked to your dad about it yet, but thought I'd call him tonight and plan the details."

"It doesn't matter anymore," she said, not looking at me.

"What do you mean?" I walked closer to her. "Did something happen?"

She stared at her screen, punching it harshly.

"Christine?"

She finally looked up. "He canceled, okay?"

"He canceled?"

"Don't act so surprised," she said. "You never wanted us to go anyway. You probably told him to cancel."

"I did not."

I said the words, but she didn't believe me. She shook her head at me.

"You ruin everything, do you know that? Everything. Dad says so too. He says you ruined your marriage. It was all your fault."

Ouch.

"Listen, honey. I know you're upset, but it isn't my fault your dad canceled. I'm sure something came up, maybe work. He's been gone for quite a while. He needs to make money at some point."

She stared at me, her jaws clenched, her nostrils flaring slightly. "It's all your fault. The divorce, the move, everything. Why did you have to ruin it? We were doing fine in Washington. I was happy there. Why did you have to change it?"

"Honey, when two people decide to…"

"Oh, don't give me that," she said with a sniffle, then slid down from her stool. "You don't care about any of us. You never even asked us if we wanted to move down here; you just decided to do it. You don't care about anyone but yourself. You're so selfish!"

"You think I'm selfish?" I said. "Your dad is the one who left. He just left us all. And now he doesn't want you anymore. He doesn't want to see you. He has moved on. He has a new woman now. He wants to marry her someday. He has a new family now. And you think I'm selfish? At least I'm here; at least I'm not going anywhere."

My daughter stared at me, her eyes wild and angry.

"You're lying! You're nothing but a selfish liar!" she yelled, then ran up the stairs. A second later, I heard the door to her room slam shut and music blasting so loud her sister started to yell for her to turn it down. In the living room, Alex knocked over something big, and it shattered with a loud crash.

I sank into a chair with a deep sigh, then hid my face between my hands, thinking it didn't matter how hard I tried; I simply couldn't win in life.

Chapter 75

AS SHE WHISTLED through the air, eyes closed, prepared to hit the water, Maddie was certain it was the end. She would most definitely die now. But as she plunged through the murky water, she felt very much alive, and soon after, she swam toward the surface.

Maddie gasped for air as she poked through and saw the blue sky above her again. She couldn't believe her luck. But as she looked back at the house behind her, where she had jumped from, she realized it wasn't over yet. Her captor was coming out the back door and rushing toward the canal.

Half in panic, Maddie started swimming. Living in Florida, most kids learned how to swim at a very young age, but Maddie hadn't had that luck. Her mom hadn't taken her to swimming lessons and, therefore, she was fairly old before she learned and wasn't among the best of swimmers. That meant she had to fight to swim fast, and it wasn't easy. Maddie whimpered while pushing her way through the dark water, trying to keep the thoughts of what lurked underneath the surface at bay.

Her captor reached the seawall and was yelling at her. Maddie panted and swam as fast as she could when she heard an engine start behind her and turned to look with a gasp. Her captor had wired his boat down from his dock and was soon rushing toward her. Maddie tried to scream but got water in her mouth and coughed instead. As she saw the boat begin to move toward her, she pushed herself even harder, trying to swim as fast as she could, panic eating at her.

Please, dear God. You've helped me get this far; please, help me get away. Please, God.

Maddie splashed in the water, panting as the boat came closer and closer. The engine roared behind her like some wild animal and Maddie was about to cry helplessly. As it came really close, and the man reached his hands down toward her, Maddie took in a deep breath, then dove down into the dark water and started to swim in the opposite direction, going underneath the boat. She kept swimming with all the strength in her small body, underneath the water, getting as far away as possible from the sound of the boat, pushing herself until she could hardly take it anymore.

Finally, she swam to the surface, then turned to look. The boat had disappeared far down the canal, and her captor hadn't realized what had happened. He was still looking down into the water, searching for her in the wrong place. It would take him a while to turn the boat around and, by then, she could be long gone.

Maddie made sure not to make a sound, then continued to swim down the canal, staying close to the seawalls and the houses. She made it down another canal, then heard an engine approaching from behind her. With a gasp, she swam underneath a dock and held onto the pillars while the boat rushed past her, the engine roaring loudly. She stayed there till it got dark and she finally dared to let go again and plunge herself into the water. As she swam again, she thought she heard a sound coming from the mangrove she had just passed and turned to look, staring straight into the eyes of an animal.

Maddie had been living in Florida most of her life and knew exactly what she was looking at.

Gator!

Frantically, Maddie splashed her arms to get away from it, then reached a dock and pulled herself out of the water just in time. She crawled onto the grass, panting in exhaustion, and lay on her stomach for a few minutes, catching her breath before realizing she couldn't stay there in case her captor came back. She had to keep moving.

Chapter 76

MY MOM HAD INVITED us for dinner so, after taking a nap, I told Alex to put on his flip-flops, then walked upstairs to get the girls. I knocked on Olivia's door and peeked inside.

"Hi there. You ready to go?"

She took off her headphones, then groaned. "Do we have to go? I can't stand the food she serves."

I sighed. "Me either, but it means a lot to Grandma and Grandpa that we come over. It was one of the reasons we moved down here. So you kids could get to know them better. Plus, it means I don't have to think about dinner tonight. It's a great help."

Olivia scoffed, then rose from her bed. "It's not like you cook anyway. We could just order pizza again."

I gave her a look. She chuckled. "Okay, okay. I'll go. But I won't eat anything."

I laughed. "That bad, huh?"

"Worse."

Olivia walked down the stairs, and I heard her talking to Alex while looking for her flip-flops. I hurried to Christine's room and knocked. The music had stopped. I hoped that meant she wasn't angry anymore.

"Christine? We're getting ready to leave."

I opened the door, and my heart dropped. She wasn't there.

"Christine?" I asked and looked in her walk-in closet and then her bathroom, but she wasn't there either.

That is odd.

I walked back into the hallway, then to the stairs, where Olivia and Alex were waiting. Their eyes rested on me.

"Are we leaving or what?" Olivia asked.

Alex had grabbed his fire ax and hat. I could tell he couldn't wait to go play with his grandpa.

"Have you seen Christine?" I asked.

Olivia shook her head. "No."

My heart started to beat faster in my chest. "She's not downstairs?"

I walked down toward them, then into the kitchen, then the living room, and finally, I checked the backyard. No sign of my daughter anywhere.

"Could she have gone to a friend's house?" Olivia asked.

"Without telling me? That's not very like her," I said. "She knows how terrified I get when I don't know where you are."

Olivia gave me a look. "Because of what happened to your sister, oh, yes, but think about it. Maybe that's exactly why she didn't say anything. To get back at you. You two were fighting earlier, right?"

"Yes, she got really mad and ran upstairs, and then…you think she snuck out while I was sleeping?" I asked.

Olivia threw out her hands. "What better way to get back at you? That's what I would do."

She was right. Christine knew how scared I got in these situations. If she really wanted me to suffer, this was the way to do it.

I grabbed my phone and called her, but she didn't pick up. "It goes directly to voicemail."

"Because she doesn't want you to find her," Olivia said.

"You try," I said. "You call her."

Olivia gave me a look. "Mo-om. First of all, don't you think she can figure out that you told me to call her? Besides, if she shut off the phone, it doesn't matter who calls."

"Then I'll just have to call everyone in her class and ask if they know where she is."

"You really think that's necessary?" Olivia asked. "Think about it. You'll only embarrass her, and she'll end up resenting you even more."

I exhaled. "Then I don't know what to do."

Olivia put her arm around my shoulder. "Relax, Mom. Let's just go to Grandma and Grandpa's; then she'll probably be here when we get home."

"Yeah," Alex said, holding out his ax in front of him. "Let's go now!"

Chapter 77

WE ALL SEEMED to be getting on each other's nerves. I don't know if it was something in the air or the food, but everyone at my mom's dinner table seemed to be grumpy.

The only one who was completely unaffected was Alex. He played with his ax around the house while my mom kept a watchful eye on him, making sure he didn't tip over any expensive antique vases or slam the toy ax into any furniture and make a dent.

I had told them that Christine was at a friend's house but found it so hard to focus on the conversation we were having while my thoughts kept circling around my daughter and where she could be. With all that had been going on, I simply didn't like not knowing where she was.

"What do you think, Eva Rae?" my mom said.

I hadn't heard what they were talking about, so I answered in confusion. "About what?"

"Dear Lord, Eva Rae, where is your mind these days?" my mom said. "I was talking about the Begonias in the front yard and how beautiful they were when they bloomed. I was wondering if I should remove the Periwinkles and make room for more. What do you think?"

I stared at her, my eyes blinking. I had no idea what to say. I couldn't care less about flowers right now. I never cared about flowers. I liked looking at them, but that was about it.

"Christine is missing," I said instead of answering her. As I said the words, tears finally escaped my eyes, and I couldn't hold it back anymore. "I don't know where she is, and I keep imagining these scenarios with all the kidnapped children lately and with Sydney and all that...I just..."

My mother stared at me, mouth gaping. Her eyes flickered a few times back and forth, and then she rose to her feet and was about to walk away.

"No, Mom," I said and grabbed her hand. "You can't go now. You always leave when..."

But my mom wouldn't hear me out; she pulled her hand away. "I have to check on the bean-flour pie," she said.

I slammed my hand onto the table, and the silverware clattered. "No, Mom! I want you to stay now. I need you to stay here and talk to me. My daughter is missing. You can't just run away from me when I tell you something like this. I need you, dammit. I need you to comfort me, to tell me it'll be all right, that she'll be fine."

My mom froze in place. She stood for a few seconds with her back turned to me, then turned around.

"I can't say that."

"Why, Mom? Why can't you say that? Why can't you, for once, comfort me when I need you to?"

She swallowed. Her nostrils were flaring. "Because...it might not be okay, Eva Rae. It wasn't for us. It never became okay again. Life was never okay again. That's why. So, forgive me if I am not very good at comforting you when things go wrong, but it is not my strong side."

She was about to turn again and leave, but I wasn't ready to let her. "Why did you never want to talk to me anymore. When it happened? Why did you freeze me out? Was it because you blame me for what happened to Sydney? Was it because you wished the kidnapper would have taken me and not her? You blame me for it, don't you? Because, believe me; I do too. Every day, I tell myself I could have done things differently and maybe saved Sydney. Because I didn't call for help early enough. Because I fought myself out of his grip and then he chose her instead. It's all my fault, isn't it, Mom? You've always believed it was. And you could never look at me the same way again. Every time I sought you, you'd turn your back on me."

My mom stood like she was frozen. Her eyes stared into mine, and her hands were shaking. I waited for her to respond. I wanted a response from her, no matter what it was. I needed to know.

She walked to me and stood so close I could smell her perfume.

"Why, Mom? Why did you have to freeze me out when I needed you the most?" I asked.

She swallowed like she needed to clear room for the words that were about to leave her mouth.

"I...I couldn't look you in the eyes, Eva Rae. I simply couldn't face you."

Tears rolled down my cheeks now, and she wiped one away.

"Why, Mom? Why not? All I wanted was a hug or a kind word?"

"Because I couldn't. I couldn't face you because I was too...ashamed."

I wrinkled my forehead. That wasn't the answer I had expected to hear from her.

"Ashamed? What on Earth are you talking about?"

My mom looked briefly at my dad, who nodded in agreement. "It's time," he said.

"Time for what? What is he talking about, Mom?" I asked, unable to stop the tears from rolling down my cheeks.

She gave me another look. Inside her eyes was the warmth

I had searched for so long, the care I knew was in there, but she never let out.

"Because I knew who took her."

It felt like she had punched me. She might as well have. I shook my head, dumbfounded.

"I…I don't understand."

"It was her father," my mother said, her voice trembling. "Her real father…your real father."

And there it was—the knockout that blew all the air out of my lungs. I heard a ringing in both my ears, and it felt like my blood had started to boil.

"Excuse me?"

My mom reached out for my hands and grabbed them in hers. Tears were in her eyes now too.

"I am so sorry, baby. I am so, so sorry."

"I…I don't understand. Dad?" I said and looked at him. I wanted him to tell me this wasn't true; I desperately needed him to tell me she was lying, to make things right again.

He nodded. "It's true, Squirt. I will always be your father because I raised you, but I am not biologically."

"We were young," my mother said. "He left. I didn't know he would come back for you. I married your father, and we decided to raise you like he was your real father because he was. You could never get a better father than him. But then he came back. Your real father did. He wanted half of the custody. We fought him in court and won. But then he…he came back, and he tried to take both of you. We saw him later on the surveillance video from the store. There was no doubt it was him. He came for both of you, sweetie, but he only got your sister."

"But…so…so, you knew who did it? All this time, you knew?"

She nodded. "The police searched for him everywhere, but they never found him. They suspected he might have taken her out of the country. He had family in Europe."

"So...so, what you're telling me is...so, she could be alive?" I said, crying. "Sydney could be alive? I thought for sure she was dead?"

My dad nodded. "We don't know if she is, but yes, there's a possibility that she is alive."

"But...how...how could you lie to me like this? I grew up thinking that...that my own mother didn't love me, that she didn't want me. And then...then you were both just...lying?"

"We did what we thought was best for you," my dad said. He said the words, but they made no sense to me.

"I have a sister out there somewhere, and a...a dad? And you thought it would be best for me not to know? What kind of logic is that?"

I stared at the man I had called my dad, suddenly feeling so confused I got dizzy. I leaned on a chair while gathering my thoughts. Everything I believed had been a lie so far. Everything. I had gone into the force because I wanted to make amends for what happened to my sister, for not being able to save her from the faceless man, her kidnapper and who I presumed was her killer. But now...now, it had all changed. And my dad? He wasn't who I believed he was, neither was my mom.

And who the heck was I?

"Eva Rae...I..." my mom said and stepped forward.

I pulled back. I needed to get away, get out of there, out of the house where I had been lied to for thirty-five years. I couldn't trust either of them anymore.

"I need to...I have to go. Come on, kids. We should get home."

Alex sighed disappointedly, while Olivia, who had watched it all play out, sprang to me and held me. I leaned on her most of the walk home, none of us uttering a word, except Alex who was pretending he was saving us all from some feisty bushfire.

Chapter 78
THEN

"COME ON, join us in the fun."

It was the third time the boy's mother urged him to come and play cards with them. But the boy still refused. He didn't think his sister should either. He thought she was being ridiculous, the way she laughed and had fun without thinking about the consequences.

"I think we need to go home now," he said. "Mom and Dad might be worried now."

"Nonsense," their mom said. "They'll be fine. Have some fun instead. You're always so serious."

The boy didn't know how long they had been in their mother's apartment, but as he watched the clock on the wall move, it made him feel more and more anxious.

It had gotten dark outside, and the boy knew his dad would most certainly be home by now. He always came home when it grew dark outside. And he would be mad if he found out where the boy and his sister were. Oh, boy, he would get so mad.

"Come on; we need a third man," his mother said. Her voice sounded strange, and he wondered if she was drunk or high. Was it just a matter of time before she hurt one of them?

Her baby sister drank from her soda and ate some gummy bears. The boy shook his head, staring at her. Didn't their mom know that little sister got too hyper when she ate all that sugar? That it wasn't good for her?

"Don't eat that," he said.

His sister grabbed another one and chewed it, loudly smacking her lips at him. He looked away. The boy walked to the window and looked outside. The darkness had settled now. There was no way he could find his way home on his own from here. Especially not in the darkness. But he had to get back somehow. He simply had to. He couldn't leave his sister here, not with her. He simply didn't dare to, so instead he snuck into the bedroom where there was an old phone on the table. He dialed his dad's number.

"Daddy?"

"Son?"

He sounded angry, and the boy's heart sank.

"Where are you?"

"I'm...I'm..." The boy began to cry. "At Mommy's place."

"What? You're at her place? She kidnapped you, son? Did she?" he asked.

"N-No..."

There was another voice on his father's end, and the boy recognized it as his new mommy's.

"What's going on?" she asked.

"The Thing kidnapped our children," his dad said. "Can you believe her?"

"Oh, dear Lord."

"I'm calling the cops," he said, then returned to the boy. "Stay where you are, son. We'll get help. Stay calm, boy, and keep a close eye on your sister. Help is on the way. Just make sure to keep an eye on your sister, you hear me?"

"Y-yes, Daddy."

Chapter 79

"CHRISTINE? CHRISTINE?"

I ran inside the house and up the stairs, then opened the door to her room. But she wasn't there. I had to control myself in order not to panic. I breathed in deeply a few times, then told myself she was fine, that she would come home soon.

"Is she still not here?" Olivia asked as she came inside her sister's room. For the first time, I now saw concern in my older daughter's eyes.

"I'll try and call her," she said, then left with her phone in hand. She came back a second later. "She's still not answering."

I ran a hand through my hair, trying hard to keep calm and to focus on where she might be.

"I'll have to call her friends now," I said, then rushed downstairs to find the list of phone numbers I had for Christine. She hadn't made a lot of friends so far, so it was quickly done.

None of them had seen her all day. Not since school.

Oh, dear God, no!

"Relax, Mom," my daughter said. "I'm sure she's fine. She might just be hiding, or maybe she went down to the beach?

Maybe she just went out because she was mad, and now she doesn't dare to come home."

I sent her a series of text messages, telling her to call me as soon as possible, then opened Mappen, the app I used to track my children, but, as suspected, it wouldn't show me where she was since it only worked if the phone was turned on. For now, it only showed me her phone's last known location, which was inside the house.

"Okay," I said. "I'll go drive around for a bit and see if I can find her. Can you stay here with Alex?"

I looked at the clock. "You know what? Instead, I think I'll call for someone to come over and be with you two. I don't like you guys being all alone."

I called Melissa, but she was out of town, she told me. She and Steve had taken a couple of days off to go camping for the weekend with the kids. They had taken them out of school. I remembered that she had already told me they were going when I called her the day before. I didn't say a word about my daughter going missing. I don't know why I didn't tell her. I guess I didn't want her to worry. Besides, I kind of still hoped Christine had just run away from home, and I would find her down on the beach or maybe wandering around downtown.

Dawn was out of the question since she was still in too bad of a condition to get out of bed, so I didn't want to bother her. Matt had enough on his plate with Elijah.

That left me with only one option. My dad.

I punched in my parents' number. It was my mom who picked up. "Eva Rae? Is that really you? I am so sorry about earlier; could we just…"

"I need to talk to Dad," I said, cutting her off. I wasn't ready to accept any of her excuses or to forgive her yet. I wasn't sure I ever would be. At least not in the state I was in right now.

"Your dad…well, he's not here right now. He left…I guess

he was upset after what happened tonight. He didn't take his cell phone. It's still here on the counter."

I closed my eyes. He was my last resort. Unless...I really didn't want to have to do this; it was the last thing I wanted to...to ask my mom for anything in this world, yet I did.

"Can you maybe help me, Mom? Can you look after the kids while I go search for Christine?"

"S-sure. I'll be right over."

Chapter 80

I LEFT without a word to my mom. I had nothing to say to her. I simply let her in, then kissed Alex and Olivia, and left, thinking that she'd have to figure things out or else Olivia would be there to help her. If it wasn't for all the kidnappings lately, I would have let Olivia babysit Alex any day, but I just didn't like leaving them alone on a day like this.

I jumped into my minivan, then drove off toward downtown. I drove through where all the small shops were, then turned around and drove past Juice N' Java and City Hall, searching all the parking lots outside and calling her name. Still, no sign of my princess. Then I drove to the beach. I parked by First Street, the closest access from where I lived, then ran through the heavy sand toward the deep, dark ocean. I kept cursing myself for not having ended things well with Christine, for fighting with her in the first place. Why did I say those things to her?

It's too late now. You've played the blame and guilt game all your life and look where it got you. Nowhere. It's time to stop.

"Christine!" I called and turned to look up toward the dunes and then back down to the water. I looked all around me, scanning the area, but it didn't help much in this darkness.

"CHRISTINE!"

Nothing but the howling wind answered. A dog barked in the distance, probably from one of the beach houses or a balcony belonging to one of the condos north of me.

"Where are you, baby girl?" I asked into the darkness.

Frustrated, I sank to my knees, then sat down in the heavy sand, head slumped between my shoulder blades. I felt so tired, so exhausted.

"Where are you?" I mumbled as tears rolled down my cheeks. As my eyes got used to the darkness, I spotted a big grey heron that was staggering along on its long skinny legs in the shallow parts of the water, looking for fish to eat.

Like he had heard my cries, Matt suddenly called. I sniffled and picked up.

"Matt?"

"I've been thinking," he said. "You might be right; it could be an inside man. I hate to say this, but while sitting here by Elijah's bedside, I keep thinking about Cooper. He had a huge crush on you back in high school and always resented me for being with you back when we dated because I knew about his crush. What if he wanted to hurt me all along? His parents are divorced; they split just last year, and he surfed with Sophie Williams down by the pier. He also helped build the senator's pool house, he told me. To earn extra money."

I exhaled, wiping tears from my eyes. "Matt…I…Christine is missing." As I said the words, I broke down, sobbing. "I think he might have her, Matt. I'm scared."

"Christine is missing? Why didn't you call me?" he asked, sounding almost angry with me.

"I don't know. I'm not very good at asking for help, I guess. But now I'm doing just that. I need you, Matt. I need your help. Please."

Chapter 81

MATT TOOK charge of the situation. He called in help from all the CBPD officers and had every patrol on the streets within the next half hour. He called Phillip at the fire station and asked them to pitch in. Luckily, Phillip wasn't holding a grudge against me and said they'd organize a search team. They'd take the trucks out and drive around in the streets and look for Christine. They even called in the only K-9 in the department, the German Shepherd, Buster—who went by the nickname *the Major*—to go through the bushy areas, the parks and areas surrounding the canals. Two officers went out on a boat to sail through all the canals in case Christine had fallen in. Patrol cruisers in the neighboring towns of Cape Canaveral and Satellite Beach were on the lookout too.

Seeing Matt work his magic made me calm down, and soon I managed to push all the desire to give up along with all the anger over what I had learned about my parents tonight aside. It had to wait.

"All right," he said and smiled at me. "I have literally everyone searching for her; even the coast guard will send out helicopters, and I've put out an Amber Alert. We'll find her. Don't you worry."

I swallowed and forced a smile. "Thanks, Matt. I mean it."

"Believe me; I want to do this. If anyone knows what you're going through right now, it's me. I want to find your daughter and hopefully also get the bastard who hurt my son and put him behind bars for the rest of his life. This is very personal for me."

I swallowed, thinking about Elijah and how close it had been. I kept imagining Christine alone and scared, crying and calling for me. It broke my heart.

"Let's go," Matt said. "We might as well get out there and look for her too."

He grabbed my hand and pulled me into a deep hug. He held me tight, then kissed the side of my head, while whispering, "We'll find her; don't worry, Eva Rae."

We both got into his police cruiser, then drove off. We drove through town once again, and I stared at all the dark empty shops, wondering if Christine could be wandering around or maybe hiding somewhere. If she really had run away from home, then maybe she was just sitting somewhere, not wanting or maybe daring to go home. But where? Where could a twelve-year-old girl hide at this time of night?

We drove down a couple of residential streets, and Matt drove past the houses slowly, so I could look out the window and see if I could spot anything out of the ordinary. The streets looked so calm, so normal. Inside all those houses, people were asleep; families were dreaming sweet dreams, sleeping heavily, the parents knowing that their kids were safe in their beds.

"I don't even know what I am looking for," I said.

"Let's just continue," Matt said and drove up Minutemen Causeway, the main street that went straight through the entire town, past the schools and ended at the country club's golf course. We drove all the way to the end of it and looked at all the residential houses down there. It was one of the wealthier areas in Cocoa Beach and the houses were bigger here and many of them facing the big river instead of small canals like the houses in my neighborhood.

Having a canal in the backyard seemed very grand, and it was really nice, but most houses in Cocoa Beach had that. River views were the ones that were more expensive, and after that came ocean views. Living on a barrier island made it possible for almost everyone to have some type of water in their backyard.

"She's not here," I said.

I grabbed my phone and held it between my hands. My eyes were fixated on the screen as I was willing it to ring and dreaming of her name appearing on the screen. Under my breath, I began praying for her to call and tell me she was sorry and to come get her.

But, of course, she didn't. The phone remained dark and lifeless.

"How about I take you back?" he said. "You haven't slept much lately and, frankly, you look like crap, no offense."

I nodded. "None taken."

"I'll keep looking, and we have literally everyone out here," he said. "You can take a nap if you want to." He reached over and put his hand on top of mine, then squeezed it. "I am not giving up till…"

I was listening to his kind words when my eyes fell on something—or rather someone— running across the street and into a yard. Matt saw it too and paused.

"What the heck was that?" he asked.

I opened the door to the cruiser. "The question is not what, it's *who,* and if I am not mistaken, the answer is a young girl."

Chapter 82

THE GIRL WAS RUNNING. She was fast, and we could barely keep up with her as we began our pursuit. I was the first one out of the cruiser, Matt coming up behind me.

"Christine?" I yelled as I reached a yard and jumped over the fence. The girl was already at the bottom of it and crawling over another fence to the neighboring house.

"Stop!" I yelled, but she didn't. She slid down into the neighboring yard, then ran across their lawn. A dog barked from inside the house. I followed her.

Why is she running away from me?

"Christine," I yelled again. "Stop. I'm not mad at you."

Christine had reached the other end of the next yard and climbed the wooden fence. She was a lot lighter than me, so she was quickly on the other side, whereas I had to fight to get up there. My hands were filled with splinters as I reached the other side, just in time to see Christine reach the next yard, pushing herself through a row of bushes. I sped up and, panting heavily, I reached the bushes and pushed my way through as well. There was a pool on the other side, and I almost fell in but managed to balance my way out of it and around it before I spotted Christine running up toward the house and trying to go back into the street. As I saw the tall wall in front of me leading to the next yard, I realized she had given up climbing it and taken an easier way out instead.

I managed to almost catch up to her, using all the strength I had, and cursing myself for not having gone on more runs since I got back here like I had promised myself.

"Christine! Stop running," I said, gasping for air. My legs were hurting and the muscles cramping from running, but I ignored it all. I had to catch up to my daughter before I lost her again, no matter the cost.

But Christine was faster than me and soon made it out to the front yard before she ran into the street. And that was when I tripped. Over a stupid sprinkler in the lawn. I fell flat on my face into the grass and, before I managed to get back to my feet, I saw her run around the corner at the end of the street.

"Oh, no, you don't," I said, then spotted a shortcut. If I ran through the yard of the corner house, I might be able to get in front of her. So, I did. I ran as fast as I ever had, through bushes that scratched me up, across a yard with a swing set and a pool, jumped a fence, and then ran into the street, right in front of her.

I held my hand out.

"Stop!"

She stopped. With gasping breath, she stared at me, her eyes blinking, terror glistening in them. Matt came up behind her, panting. I stared at the girl, my heart beating hard.

It wasn't Christine.

I walked closer, and a deep furrow grew between my eyes as I realized who she was.

"Maddie?"

"I'm not going back," she said, crying, then looked at Matt standing behind her. "I'm not."

I reached out my hand and shook my head. "Of course not, sweetie. We're the police. You're safe with us."

She stared at me, her eyes revealing doubt in my words.

"It's okay," I said and bent down to seem less frightening to her. "We've been looking for you. I am so glad to see you, and your mother will be too when we tell her we've found you. She's been really worried."

Maddie's face softened. Her eyes were still skeptical. "You know my mom?"

I nodded. "Her name is Patricia, right? She's been so worried. We all have. Even Mrs. Altman who lives downstairs. She was the one who took a picture of the car that picked you up. If you'll let me. I'll take you to your mother right now."

Maddie stared into my eyes and then it was like the air went out of her completely. She started to cry and threw herself into my arms. I lifted her up and carried her to the cruiser, happy to have found her, but secretly wishing it had been my daughter instead.

Chapter 83
THEN

THE POLICE CAME with sirens and blinking lights on their cars. The boy watched them drive up into the street in front of his mother's condominium. His baby sister and their mother were still playing cards and eating candy, laughing like nothing bad had happened, like what they were doing wasn't wrong. For a second, as the boy watched the policemen running toward the house, guns drawn, he regretted having done what he did, having called his dad, but then he reminded himself that his mother was a bad person, that she was the one who had abandoned him; she was the one who had acted crazy and not come when she was supposed to pick him up. She was the one who had chosen the drugs over him; she was the one who used to hurt him, and she was the one who chose that bad life over him and his sister. She was the one who couldn't be trusted, and they weren't safe here with her.

No, it was the right thing to do, to call his dad. And if Dad thought it was a situation that called for the police, then that was what was best for him and his sister. His mother was a dangerous person who had kidnapped them, and now she was going to pay for that.

There was a knock on the door, and then it was kicked in. That was when the yelling began. The boy watched in determination as the smiles finally froze on his mother's and sister's faces. Finally, they realized the seriousness of the situation.

"POLICE! GET DOWN TO THE GROUND. NOW!"

The boy threw himself to the carpet and turned to look as his mother started to scream, holding both hands to her face, when an officer pulled his baby sister out of her grasp.

"NO! You can't do that! She's my child! You can't take my child! Please…"

Two officers held her down while she screamed and yelled, becoming the crazy mommy that the boy had seen and knew she really was deep inside. She screamed so loudly that the officers pointed their guns at her and suddenly she somehow ripped herself out of their grasp and stormed toward his baby sister, ripped the child out of the hands of the officer, and tried to run with her when the officers yelled at her to stop. They reached out to grab her, but she zigzagged her way away from them. When she didn't stop, one of them fired his gun at her as she rushed for the back door, holding baby sister in her arms. But as he did that, the boy's mother turned around in a scream, and the bullet hit baby sister instead.

The boy couldn't breathe as he watched his mommy tumble to the ground, three officers on top of her, tackling her, baby sister falling out of her grip, and falling lifelessly to the ground, bleeding from the wound in her chest.

"NOOO! MY BABY, NOOO!" Mommy screamed while the boy gasped for air. He then felt hands on his body and was lifted into the air and, while screaming and kicking, he was carried out into a car and strapped in. He stared at the building in front of him, screaming and hammering on the window until he spotted baby sister being rushed into an ambulance and taken away from the scene.

The boy never saw her again. She went into cardiac arrest in the ambulance and died on her way to the hospital, he was later told.

As the boy was finally taken back to his home and to Dad and New Mommy, they hugged him very tightly and told him he had done what he could, but the woman was crazy, and she had killed his baby sister. She was the one to blame. The Thing was to blame, and she would end up spending a long time in jail for what she had done. At least it was over now, and the woman would be gone for many years. He would never have to see her again.

Ever.

Chapter 84

WE DROVE Maddie to her mother's apartment and rang the doorbell. Patricia opened the door, her eyes red-rimmed. As they landed on her daughter, it was hard for me to keep my own tears back.

"Maddie! Is that really you? Oh, heaven have mercy; I can't believe it!"

Patricia almost screamed the words out, then grabbed her daughter in her arms and held onto her and kissed her face while Maddie laughed. I was smiling, joyful over having been able to bring her daughter back, but inside I was screaming in pain, wishing terribly that this was me, that I too would get to hold and kiss my daughter again until she screamed for me to stop.

"Let me look at you, baby," Patricia said and held her daughter's face between her hands. "Are you hurt?"

Maddie shook her head.

"Thank God," her mother exclaimed and hugged her again. She gave me a look and mouthed a *thank you*.

"You're welcome," I whispered back, then raised my voice to normal volume, choking back my own tears. "But more children are missing, and we need to speak to Maddie about where she has been and what she saw."

"Does it have to be right now?" Patricia asked.

"I am afraid so," Matt said. "The sooner we talk to her about these things, the better her recollection will be, and the better our chances are to find the other girl we believe he is holding captive."

"Yes, well, come on in," Patricia said. "I'll make some mac and cheese; are you hungry, Maddie?"

She nodded, and I could tell Maddie was wearied. All the adrenaline from running from her captor was almost gone now, and she would soon be overwhelmed with exhaustion.

We went inside and sat down. Patricia served us some coffee, and I held Maddie's hands in mine. Her skin was smooth and soft like Christine's.

"What can you tell us, Maddie?" I asked. "You told us in the car that you were held captive, but you escaped. What can you tell us about the place you were kept? Were there any other children there?"

She nodded while her mother found a box of mac and cheese and microwaved it.

"There were. Do you know who?" I asked, my heart beating fast.

Maddie shook her head. "I never got to see who it was, but there was someone there. In a box."

"Elijah," Matt said, and our eyes met. This confirmed that Maddie had been held by the same guy that had taken Matt's son, the same guy who said he had killed Sophie Williams, Scott Paxton, and Nathaniel Pullman, the senator's son. We didn't know what his plans with Maddie were, but it looked like they were interrupted by Maddie running away, which was good.

"Who else?" I asked. "Was there another girl there?"

Maddie looked at me, then shook her head. "No."

My heart dropped. "Oh, okay. And you're sure about that?"

She nodded with a sniffle. She was so tired now that her face was turning pale. She wouldn't be able to hold on for much longer. We had to hurry and get all the information out of her that we could.

"What about your kidnapper?" Matt asked. "Did you know him?"

She nodded her head while her mother served her the food. "He used to come here and bring us food."

I looked at her mother for answers. "The church. They send us food from time to time when I sign up for it."

Maddie nodded. "There was one guy who came several times."

"Do you know his name?" I asked.

Her mother shook her head. "There have been so many."

Maddie began to eat, and I realized the girl had probably barely eaten for days.

"I was blindfolded most of the time, but I managed to see a little anyway, that's how I saw the nail that helped me get loose."

"So, you saw his face," I said.

She nodded with her mouth full.

"But you don't know where we can find him?" Matt continued.

She shook her head.

"But you said you jumped into a canal, so that must mean the house was one of the canal houses, and there was a pool, you said?"

She nodded. "Yes. A big one."

"Lots of houses around here have pools and are on the canals," Matt said with a sigh.

"Still, it's getting us closer," I said and looked at the girl. "Try and think back. Was there anything about the place that you remember? Anything that stood out?"

She chewed, then swallowed and nodded. "There was a name. It was scratched into the wall. I was guessing one of the other girls had done it, one that had been there before me."

"A name?" I asked. "What name was that?"

"Sydney," she said and shoveled in another spoonful of mac and cheese while my heart stopped beating. I stared at her.

"S-Sydney?"

She nodded, chewing.

"And you're sure that's what it said?" Matt asked, giving me a concerned look.

Maddie nodded.

"I think I need to get her to bed," her mother said. "She's exhausted and, frankly, so am I. I got a new job at the pharmacy and need to be up early. Can we continue the rest tomorrow?"

Matt nodded and got up. I was staring at the girl, while it felt like a thousand pieces of a puzzle fell into place in my mind. It made no sense, but something was beginning to add up.

"We're done here anyway," Matt said. "Right, Eva Rae?"

I steadied my breath and calmed myself down, then rose to my feet as well. "Yes, we're done."

As we walked to the car, Matt looked at me. "Are you okay?"

I swallowed, pressing the anxiety and fear back. "Yes, yes. I'm fine. Just tired, that's all."

"I meant from hearing your sister's name like that. It must be a shock. Do you think it's the same guy who took your sister back then?"

I walked to the door of the cruiser and grabbed the handle. "I...I have no idea. I just want to go home now. And take that nap we talked about. I can't even see straight anymore."

Matt nodded. "Sure. I'll keep in touch with the search crews and let you know as soon as we find her, and we will find her, you hear me?"

I strapped myself in, nodding. "I heard you. And I believe you. Now, take me home, please."

Chapter 85

HE DROPPED me off in the driveway, and I thanked him, then waved and watched him drive away. As soon as he reached the end of the road, I took one glance at my house, then left, walking down the street. Walking soon became running and, a few minutes later, I was standing in front of a house with a swimming pool and a canal in the backyard. I walked around it, kicked the back door in and walked inside, holding my gun out in front of me.

Quietly, I walked to the stairwell, then rushed up the stairs and down the hallway. I stood in front of the white door, my heart thumping in my chest. I tried to turn the knob, but it was locked. I kicked it open, not caring that I broke it, thinking I'd have to deal with this later.

I walked into the room and found it completely barren— no furniture and nothing on the walls except for black foam. I walked to the end of it and found small splinters on the carpet.

From a wooden box.

Then I spotted the words on the wall and walked closer, reaching out my hand to touch them.

"Sydney," I mumbled. A flood of images from the day she

had been taken away from me rushed through my mind. I pushed them back, deciding this wasn't the time for me to get mushy and emotional.

I looked around me, searching for any trace of Christine having been here too, then when I didn't find any, I left the room. I searched the rest of the house but didn't find any trace of her there either. Disappointed, I found a stationary computer inside an office and pressed the spacebar. I searched around on it for a little while and found first the video of Elijah that had been sent to Matt, then the video of Sophie and Nathaniel. I found the original videos of them as well and the program he had used to edit them. Then, I found a document and opened it.

Up came a list of names and plans for how to kill them and place them. I saw Sophie Williams' name on top, then followed the senator's son and then Elijah, then Maddie, who was supposed to have been strangled then placed at the house of a famous politician who lived in Satellite Beach, who had often frequented Maddie's mother. A total humiliation for all involved. Next on the list was the name of a boy I didn't recognize. But there was something else.

An address.

Chapter 86

RYLAN HAD TO PEE. It was the middle of the night, and he and Faith had been sleeping with their mommy.

He held his nose as he sat up straight, feeling woozy from sleeping near the bad smell. He blinked his eyes a few times to make sure he wasn't seeing things. As he looked again, he knew he wasn't. Someone was there, sitting in a chair and watching him.

"W-who are you?" he asked.

The man smiled. Between his hands, he was holding a gun. The sight made Rylan gasp. He hadn't seen one in real life before, only on TV. It looked smaller in real life than on the screen. But just as dangerous.

"I'm here to help you," the man replied.

Rylan looked away, then glanced carefully at his mother and sleeping sister. "Help me with what?"

The man scoffed. "How's your mommy? Huh?"

Rylan swallowed. "She's fine. She'll wake up soon. She just needed to sleep; that's all."

"How's that going for you, huh? Taking care of yourself and your sister while she sleeps, huh?"

Rylan breathed heavily. "Fine."

"It's tough, am I right? Taking care of a sibling. You are all alone."

Rylan bit his lip. "I can do it."

"Can you?" the man said

The boy nodded. He felt like crying but knew he couldn't. Not while the man was looking. He had to be strong now. For Faith and for his mother's sake. Rylan had heard stories about Timmy from third grade who had been taken away from his mother because she couldn't take proper care of him. Rylan knew his mother would take care of him as soon as she woke up. Everything would go back to normal. As soon as she…

"You know she's dead, don't you?" the man suddenly said.

Rylan stared at the man, his upper lip shaking. He was biting his tongue, so he wouldn't cry but had to bite so hard that he soon tasted blood.

"You're lying! She'll wake up soon."

The man winked. "You really believe that?"

The boy breathed, his nostrils flaring. But he didn't answer. Because, deep down, he knew the man was right. As the realization slowly sunk in, Rylan began to cry, finally allowing himself to let it all out. The tears rushed down his cheeks while his young body shook with the effort of trying to hold them back.

"Come on, Rylan. Don't lie to me. You know that she's dead, don't you? She has been for a long time."

The boy tried hard to fight his desire to yell and scream at the man, tell him he was a mean liar and that everything would change when she woke up, and to go away. He didn't dare to because the man was still holding the gun, yet despair was filling Rylan with such overwhelming force, he didn't really know what to do with it, how to make it go away.

"So, now it's just you and Faith, I guess," the man said. "Can you take care of her? For the rest of your life? Are you man enough for that?"

Rylan sobbed and wiped his nose with the back of his

hand. The man's words hurt him deeply, and he realized he had no idea how to take care of his sister anymore. They had survived so far, but only because he believed his mommy would wake up soon.

There was no way he could do this any longer.

He shook his head. "N-No."

The man rose to his feet, then said, "I think I can help you avoid that."

He then stretched out his hand holding the gun.

Chapter 87

I SLAMMED my hand into the steering wheel, cursing myself for being so stupid, then parked the car in the parking lot outside of the condominiums in the north part of town. I looked at the number that I had written down, then spotted the entrance and rushed up to the second floor. I knocked but didn't expect anyone to answer. There was a distinct smell in the hallway that made me want to gag. I held my sleeve up in front of my mouth, then grabbed my gun and grabbed the doorknob. The door was locked. I kicked it in, thinking I'd have to explain later how I believed someone had died in there because of the smell and that I believed two young children's lives were in danger.

I was right about both assumptions. As I walked inside, I found the boy standing in the bedroom.

"Police!" I yelled and walked closer.

The boy didn't move. He was staring at something and, as I entered the room, first looking around to make sure the children were alone, I realized he was watching a woman I could only assume was his mother. She was lying in the bed, flies in her dead staring eyes. Next to her lay a young child, a girl, sleeping heavily.

"Are you Rylan?" I asked and turned to face the boy. He whimpered and nodded, and that was when I realized he was holding a gun between his hands.

"What are you doing with that gun, Rylan?" I asked.

The boy answered with sobs. "I can't do it," he said.

"What can't you do?" I asked.

"Take care of her."

I looked at the girl on the bed. She was awake now and staring at us both. "You mean your sister? Her name is Faith, right?"

He nodded. "And you have been taking care of her? Of the both of you. Because your mom died?"

He nodded again, then sobbed and sniffled. Tears ran down his small chubby cheeks. He could be no more than four or five years old, his sister maybe two. I put my gun back in the holster, then knelt in front of him.

"Just hand me the gun, Rylan. You don't want to hurt anyone, do you?"

"You know that many kids who go through a divorce end up taking care of their siblings?" a voice said behind me.

The floor creaked under his heavy feet as he moved closer. I knew the sound of his steps like my own heartbeat.

"It's sad when you think about it. The older child has to become a parent because the parents can no longer take proper care of them. Forces them to grow up too fast."

I heard the gun cock behind my head and raised my hands in the air.

"It happened to you, didn't it?" I asked. "You had to take care of your sister when your parents split?"

"Good detective work," he said.

I turned to look at him. "But she died, didn't she? Your mom killed her. That's what you told me when I was a kid. That was why you never had any contact with her. Because of what happened back then."

My dad nodded. "I thought I had it all figured out. My

mom was the bad guy. She was a drug addict, she was crazy, she couldn't take care of us, and she tried to kidnap us. That's what we were told. That's what we believed."

I swallowed. "But that wasn't the entire story, was it?"

He shook his head. "I didn't know till she died last year. I hadn't seen her since the day she was taken away when my sister died. I never wanted to know of her for my entire adult life, not even when I heard she was released from prison. I never wanted to see her again. But then they called from the nursing home she had been living before she died and told me she was gone and that they had a box of her stuff they didn't know what to do with. My initial thought was to leave it there to rot, but then I thought maybe I should burn it all, get rid of every tie to her once and for all. As they gave me the boxes, I couldn't help but go through them. And that was when I found the letters. Letters she had written to me while in prison but gotten back unopened. Letters explaining everything in detail. All my life, I had been told she didn't want me, that she forgot about my sister and me and didn't show up on days when she was supposed to have us, but it was all a lie. My father had deliberately given her wrong dates and then told us she would come on days she wasn't supposed to. So, we would wait for her for hours and stare out the window waiting for her to come. That way, he built up anger in us toward her, and it drove her crazy. So, when she came to see us unannounced, she ended up being angry and aggressive because she was sad and frustrated. She wanted to see us, she wanted us, and all that time, my dad told me that she didn't want us. She had fought for us, but when we went to court, my dad had told us to say we didn't want to be with her. He told the judge my mother was on drugs, but she never was, never touched the stuff. She never hurt me. It all came back to me as I read the letters. My dad would tell us how she would beat us, but I don't remember her hurting my sister or me even a single time. She loved us. She loved me, and I lost all those years. I could have had a mother. My dad and his new wife brainwashed us into thinking she was this terrible person, that she was dangerous for us when she wasn't. It was all a darn lie."

"They alienated you from her, so you didn't even want to see her," I said.

"Don't you get it? It was my fault. I did it," my dad said, a tear escaping the corner of his eye. His next words came out as choked sobs, "I lost her. I was the one who killed my sister. I called the police on my own mother and sent her to jail. Just because of some lie, some freakin lie."

"And now, they're all dead, so you can't even confront them," I said, fighting my own tears. I looked at Rylan, who was staring at the gun between his hands. Right now, all I wanted was to make sure he and his sister made it out of here alive. I had to keep my dad's focus away from the boy.

"So, you came up with this." I stared at my dad, shaking my head. "You're sick, do you know that? Killing all those children. Just to tell the world your story? What kind of a warped mind does that? I guess I should have figured it out sooner; I guess I just refused to face it. The mustache, the blue BMW. Instead, I came up with excuses, thinking lots of people own blue convertible BMWs and have mustaches. But there was also the green paint on my carpet; the same paint used to paint the side of the box that Matt's son was in. I should've guessed it then. It wasn't until Maddie told me about the name by the floorboard. I remembered it from Sydney's old room. You kept them in there. Cleared it all out without mom knowing it, and then made it into a prison. You even sound-proofed it with foam on the walls. You knew mom would never go anywhere near that room. And she certainly wouldn't let anyone else. So, you made it ready while mom visited her friends in Winter Park and went golfing with them, and you planned everything without her even suspecting a thing. You have volunteered for years as a leader with the Girl Scouts, so even if you didn't go on the campout yourself, you knew where they went and when to grab her. And what about Scott Paxton, huh? The kid you dismembered and used only his legs and arms?"

"He was just a random kid I picked up in a poor area," he said. "He wasn't important. A prop, if you will. I just needed his body parts. You'll find the rest of him in a dumpster in Titusville."

I shuddered. To think of all the times I had left him alone with my children. All the times I had been to their house, and he had been keeping those children right up there in Sydney's room while we were hanging out downstairs eating dinner. The thought made me sick.

"You and Senator Pullman go way back, and you play poker with him from time to time, at his house where you met his son, am I right?" I continued. "You stole Thomas Price's car from his mother's house to lead us to believe he killed Sophie, then used it while dumping the body of Sophie and for kidnapping Maddie from her bus stop. Patricia told me earlier that she knew you because you had often brought them groceries when they were in need. Through your volunteering job at the church, you bring food to many poor people around here, and you took especially good care of them, didn't you? Got to know them well, so when you drove up to Maddie, she believed she could trust you. But I don't know how you knew Matt had a son?"

My dad smiled. "As I told you, I know everything around here. His mom told me when I met her one day and offered her a coffee. She was devastated because Matt wasn't allowed ever to see him, and she wanted to get to know her grandchild too. It didn't take me long to find him."

"And so, you pretended to be a journalist from *Florida Today* and, being the charmer that you are, Lisa naturally believed you. And what about Rylan and Faith? How did you choose them?" I asked.

"I ran into them coincidentally. I was driving down A1A when I spotted two little children on their own, playing outside this building. I stopped and asked them where their mom was. They told me she was in bed, that she was sick and sad. I asked them where their dad was, and they said he had left. Didn't take me long to decide they would be perfect for my final act."

"And just what is your final act, Dad?" I asked.

"Well, you followed me here, didn't you? So, I guess you get to witness it. You weren't a part of my plan when I began this. I tried to stop you, to tell you to stay out of it, but you had to get yourself involved. So, now you're in it. I led you here on purpose, just like I led you to my other artwork. I never meant for you to get hurt, but you leave me no choice. You know I loved you as if you were my own, don't you? I always saw you and Sydney as mine."

"I know you did, Dad. But, please, you don't have to kill any more people. You've proved your point. Please, just let us go, will you?"

"But I'm not done," my dad said matter-of-factly. He glanced above my head at Rylan.

"You can do it, boy. Put an end to it."

Rylan looked up at him, tears streaming across his cheeks, the gun shaking in his hands.

"Rylan, no," I said. "Please, Dad, don't make him do it. Why are you this way? Why do you have to hurt people? I thought I knew you."

"Do you know how many kids commit suicide because of divorce?" my dad asked me.

I shook my head. "No, Rylan, please, just put down the gun. You don't have to do this. You have a good life ahead of you."

"No, you don't," my dad said, hissing. "Feel the pain inside of you? It'll follow you for the rest of your life. It will never leave you; it will eat at you every day you're alive, and the loneliness will grow bigger and bigger till it explodes and you either kill yourself or somebody else. Just pull the trigger. Get it over with now, Rylan; come on, boy!"

Rylan cried, then placed the tip of the gun on his nose. I stared at him with wide open eyes as his small finger slipped on the trigger and he sobbed.

"Come on, boy! Try again."

"No, Rylan, stop it," I said.

The boy was crying, his small body trembling. I looked up at my dad, who stared at the boy in anticipation. He forgot to keep an eye on me for just a short second, and I saw my chance. With a swift movement, I reached up and grabbed the gun my dad was holding, then wrestled it out of his hands. The gun was sent flying across the room, and soon my dad and I were in a fist battle on the floor.

Unfortunately for me, my dad was a lot heavier and a lot stronger, and soon he managed to throw a punch to my jaw that made my ears ring. I kicked him in the groin, and he moaned in pain when I heard a gun go off.

Chapter 88

RYLAN!

My dad fell flat on top of me. While trying to get him off of me, I turned my face to look and spotted the boy. He was still standing next to us, holding the gun between his hands, staring at something behind me. I turned to the other side and spotted Matt, standing in the doorway, holding the smoking gun between his hands.

He ran to me and helped pull my dad off me. I touched my face and wiped my dad's blood away. Matt had shot him in the back of his head. Matt reached out his hand for me to grab it.

"Are you all right?"

I took in a couple of ragged breaths, trying to get a grasp of everything, letting it all sink in.

"That depends. Physically, I think I'm fine, yes. Emotionally is a completely different conversation. How much did you hear?"

Matt shook his head. "Not much, but enough to know he was trying to kill both you and the boy. Was he...?"

I nodded. "Yes, Daddy Dearest...I guess...was our killer all along." I sighed and rubbed my forehead. So many thoughts were rushing through my mind that I couldn't really focus. The initial shock was wearing off, and soon reality would set in.

"I'll explain everything later," I said. "Right now, I need to do something."

I walked to Rylan, then knelt in front of him once again. He sniffled and looked up at me. I reached out my hand toward him, and he hesitated for just a second, then placed the gun in it. I then reached out my arm and pulled him into a hug, while Matt called for assistance.

Once he was done, he came back to me. "Maybe we should take the children outside to wait?" he said. "This place stinks, and my eyes are watering."

We did. We walked into the hallway, Matt carrying Faith in his arms. She cried as we sat down on the stairs outside, rubbing her eyes, asking what had happened. Rylan grabbed her hand in his and sat with her, holding his arm around her shoulder while explaining to her that their mommy wasn't going to wake up anytime soon.

"He killed her a few days ago," I said, addressed to Matt after a few minutes. "And the children have lived alone all this time, taking care of themselves. Just like my dad had to take care of his own sister after his parents' divorce. His sister ended up dying, though. This was all his way of telling his story, of going through his own childhood pain, killing his way through it in a very disturbed way. I can't believe I...that my...dad would do such a thing. I thought I knew him. But after tonight, I realized I didn't know him at all. I'm sorry for not involving you once I realized it had to be him. I had to be certain before I started accusing him of anything."

"I get it," Matt said. "It was something you felt like you needed to do on your own. It was your family. But, luckily for you, I knew you were up to something. I know you. Better than you think. I know you would never go back and sleep when your daughter was missing. After I dropped you off, I followed you as you ran to your parents' house and then waited outside until you came back out and ran back for your car. I followed you here but didn't want to come in at first. I had no idea what you were doing in there until it took too long, and I finally decided to go after you, thinking something had to be wrong. I'm glad I did."

I smiled up at him, and he put his arm around me.

"So am I."

I sighed deeply, trying to shake tonight's events when my thoughts once again landed on Christine. She hadn't been in Sydney's old room. She hadn't been on his list of victims, and he hadn't mentioned her.

If my dad hadn't taken her, then where was she?

Chapter 89

THE NIGHT BECAME PAINFULLY long and, as morning broke, I was finally able to leave the site and go home. Rylan and Faith were in the hands of the DCF and would be sent to live with their grandparents in Wisconsin, they told me.

My mom was sound asleep on the couch when I came back inside. She woke up as I sat down on the coffee table she had once given me. She blinked her eyes.

"Eva Rae, we don't sit on the tables," she said. "That's what we have chairs for..."

The look in my eyes made her stop.

"You didn't find her?" she asked and jolted upright.

I shook my head. I grabbed her hands between mine. "Mom. We need to talk."

"Talk? What about? Don't tell me it's about what happened last night; I know it was..."

I shook my head. "That's not what this is about. We'll get to that later. Right now, I need to tell you something that will completely shake your world, but you have to listen to me and let me finish, okay?"

My mom's eyes grew wide. "O-okay. But could we at least get a little coffee to wash this down with...whatever it is?"

"Deal."

I made the coffee, and we talked for hours. It was Saturday, so the kids didn't have school. I had to repeat a lot of it because my mom refused to believe it. But, little by little, it sunk in and soon my mom sat in my kitchen, crying and shaking her head.

"You think you know people...you live with them for years and years, and...it's all a lie?"

There were so many things I could have said at that moment to make her feel terrible about herself and how she had lied to me through all my life, but I decided against it. I realized I was no longer as angry about it as I had been. We were in this together.

"So...what will happen next?" she asked.

"Your house will be a part of the investigation," I said. "It's a crime scene now. Which means you'll have to live here for as long as it'll take them, God help us all."

"I heard that, Eva Rae," my mom said. In her voice, I heard a sort of relief. I wondered if she would ever want to go back to that place. Maybe staying here with me wasn't such a terrible idea after all. We both had to lick our wounds and find a way to move on past this. I knew we would drive each other nuts in the process, but the fact was, we needed each other.

I served my mom some cinnamon buns that I quickly baked, and she ate them without even talking about sugar or fat or cholesterol or asking if they were vegan or gluten-free. It was a relief to just be sitting there with my mom, and just be. Be human.

Barely had I finished my second bun when my phone buzzed.

"Ms. Eva Rae Thomas?" a voice asked from the other end.

"Yes?"

"TSA agent Frances Lopez, from Orlando airport here. I have someone who would like to talk to you."

"Mom?"

"Christine?"

"Oh, Mom, I..." she broke down and cried. I couldn't hold it back myself either.

"Where are you, baby? I'll come get you now. Just tell me where you are, and I'll be there."

"I'm...I'm at the airport," she said.

"Oh, baby girl. Stay where you are. I'll be right there."

I looked at my mom as I hung up. She smiled. "Well, what are you waiting for, Eva Rae? Go. I'll be here when the kids wake up."

I kissed her cheek. "Thanks, Mom."

"Just don't make a habit of it. I'm not a babysitter, you know," she shouted after me, but I was already gone.

Chapter 90

"CHRISTINE?"

I spotted her in the room that the TSA agent led me into while telling me that they had picked her up when she tried to purchase a ticket with my credit card.

Christine looked up at me, her eyes big and swollen from crying. "Oh, Mom, I'm..."

I knelt down and hugged her tightly. "No, baby. I'm the one who's sorry. I never meant to get so angry at you. I never meant to say those things. I am so, so sorry. You were trying to purchase a ticket to go see your dad, weren't you? To go to Washington?"

She nodded, crying. "Yes, but Mom, you were right. I took a shuttle to the airport and called dad and told him I was on my way, but then he said he couldn't have me. That I had to stay with you. That this wasn't a good time. I even told him I had quarreled with you and that I wanted to come live with him, but he said he didn't want that. I decided to go anyway and thought I could just crash at Amy's place instead until I convinced him to take me in. I didn't dare to come back to you. But you were right, Mom. He doesn't want us anymore."

It broke my heart, and I couldn't stop crying. "Oh, dear baby. I am so sorry."

"Why is he being like that, Mom?"

"I...I don't know, honey. Dad's going through something."

"But...can't he do that without hurting us? His children?" she asked.

I pulled her into my arms. "I don't know, sweetie. All I know is that we need to stick together. We have to help each other get through this. And I promise to try and be home a lot more, okay?"

Christine got up and grabbed my hand in hers. "Good," she said with a sniffle. "Because I can't take care of Alex all on my own anymore. He's exhausting."

We walked out the door, and I smiled at the agent before we found the exit. "Well, I might have a solution for that," I said as we walked back into the parking lot.

"Really? What?"

"Grandma is moving in with us. At least for a little while. Isn't that neat?"

My daughter stopped as we reached the car. She stared at me. "Grandma? Does that mean we all have to become vegan?"

"Okay, so we haven't figured out all the details yet, but we'll get to that eventually. Now, let's get home, baby. It's been a long day."

Chapter 91

"CAN WE OPEN OUR EYES YET?"

Olivia sounded annoyed, but I wasn't going to rush it just because of her. I wanted it to be perfect.

I corrected the board one more time, then said, "All right, you can look."

All three kids opened their eyes and stared at the white-board in front of them that I had hung up on the wall in the kitchen. Behind them, my mom was whistling as she was preparing another odd dish for us for tonight. I was eternally happy she was there and that she was cooking for us, but I was getting pretty fed up with beans and lentils by now. I just didn't want to tell her how much we all loathed her food. I didn't want to break her heart. It had been broken so much already.

"Is that it?" Alex groaned. "I thought it was something cool."

"What's this?" Christine asked. "What are we looking at?"

"This, my children, is our new organizer board. See how I put all the days here and then all the hours there? This is where you write your activities down. Like Olivia has Volley-ball on Tuesdays."

"Mondays and Wednesdays, Mom," Olivia grumbled.

"Yes, okay, Monday and Wednesday," I said and wrote it on the board. "See? Now we all know where Olivia is between three and five o'clock on Mondays and Wednesdays. And if she has a game on Saturday, then she'll write it there, and we'll all know where she is, and where I'll probably be too because I will want to see all her games this season."

Olivia rolled her eyes. "Really, Mom? Do you have to?"

I smiled. "Yes, and I will be cheering from the sidelines. Probably wearing a funny hat or something embarrassing. And maybe Grandma will want to go too?"

"Leave me out of this," my mom said. "I'll only come if sweet Olivia invites me."

"There you go," Olivia said. "Grandma understands how it works."

"Very well, but I plan on coming anyway. And I'll be at all your concerts, Christine, and your surfing contests, Alex, once you get to that level. Are we clear? Activities go on the board, and you remember to text me every now and then and you always, always pick up when I call, okay?"

"This is turning into a prison," Olivia said and walked away, probably rolling her eyes once again.

"What do you think?"

I looked at Christine for some sort of recognition. "It's okay...for you."

"I'll take that as an acknowledgment," I said and turned just in time to see Alex draw a huge fire truck all over my schedule.

"Oh, no, Alex. I spent a long time making this."

My son smiled and admired his artwork. "It looks much better now, Mom," he said, very visibly proud.

I chuckled and put a hand on his shoulder. "I can't argue with that."

· · ·

Later that same evening, I was watching TV with my mom when there was a knock on the door. I went to open it.

"Matt?"

He looked at me nervously and, at first, I feared something was wrong.

"So, here's the deal," he said. "My mom can babysit Elijah this Friday."

I looked at him, puzzled.

"And?"

He was obviously looking for words. When he didn't find them, he walked up to me, grabbed me, and pulled me into a kiss.

"You annoy the heck out of me, Eva Rae Thomas," he whispered as our lips parted.

"Odd thing to say after kissing a girl," I said, still confused.

He shook his head, almost angrily. "Don't you get it?"

"I'm not sure I do, no."

He growled something, then turned around, then returned and looked at me. "Can we try? Please? I know it didn't work out the first time, but can we try again?"

I swallowed, and a smile spread across my lips.

"Is that your way of asking me out?"

He threw out his arms. "Yes!"

"This Friday?"

"Yes!"

I shook my head. "Matt...I can't..."

"Oh, okay. Wow," he said and stepped away from me, his voice turning shrill. "But that's okay. That's okay. At least I tried, right?"

He turned around and was about to walk away when I stopped him.

"Matt, I can't...this Friday. I've promised Melissa and Dawn I'll go out with them. Some local band is playing at the Beach Shack. They're all excited to take me there. But if you can get your mom to babysit on Saturday, then I'll be delighted to."

Matt's face lit up. "Really?"

"Really."

"Yes!" he said, walking backward toward his car. "You've got it. I'll pick you up, right here. That's a date. It's a date!"

Matt got into the car and drove off, while I wondered if he was ever going to tell me what time he would pick me up. I shrugged and decided he'd probably text me, then went back inside where my mom was watching CSI Miami. I decided I wasn't in the mood for any more mystery in my life, then went into the kitchen, opened my laptop, and began to write the first page of my book.

Only, as soon as I had written the first line, I suddenly had a new idea. A story was asking to be let out and felt more urgent than the first one I had wanted to write.

The story of a boy turned killer. The story of the man I had once believed was my dad.

THE END

Afterword

Dear Reader,

Thank you for purchasing *Don't Lie to Me.*

The idea for this book came to me when I spoke to a good friend of mine who is going through a tough divorce right now.

Her husband is alienating the children against her, so they refuse to see her. He is telling them lies about her, and they believe him, mostly because they are afraid of him.

It's an awful thing and happens a lot more than you'd think. When I researched it, I found so many stories like my friend's, you wouldn't believe it. Some children don't realize this has happened to them before they are grown up and they have lost contact with one parent.

It devastated my heart to think that some parents won't get to see their own children and, not only that, their young hearts are turned against them. It's tough.

I hope you liked the book and will leave a review. It means so much to me.

Thank you for all your support,

Willow

To be the first to hear about new releases and bargains from Willow Rose, sign up below to be on the VIP List. (I promise not to share your email with anyone else, and I won't clutter your inbox.)

- GO HERE TO SIGN UP TO BE ON THE VIP LIST:
http://readerlinks.com/l/415254

Tired of too many emails? Text the word: "willowrose" to 31996 to sign up to Willow's VIP text List to get a text alert with news about New Releases, Giveaways, Bargains and Free books from Willow.

Win a signed paperback of your choice from Willow Rose! Just become a member of my Facebook group **WILLOW ROSE - MYSTERY SERIES**.
We'll randomly select a winner from all the entries.
To enter, just tap/click here: WILLOW ROSE-MYSTERY SERIES FACEBOOK CLUB.

About the Author

Willow Rose is a multi-million-copy best-selling Author and an Amazon ALL-star Author of more than 80 novels. Her books are sold all over the world.

She writes Mystery, Thriller, Paranormal, Romance, Suspense, Horror, Supernatural thrillers, and Fantasy.

Willow's books are fast-paced, nail-biting page-turners with twists you won't see coming. That's why her fans call her The Queen of Plot Twists.

Several of her books have reached the Kindle top 10 of ALL books in the US, UK, and Canada. She has sold more than three million books all over the world.

Willow lives on Florida's Space Coast with her husband and two daughters. When she is not writing or reading, you will find her surfing and watch the dolphins play in the waves of the Atlantic Ocean.

Tired of too many emails? Text the word: "willowrose" to 31996 to sign up to Willow's VIP Text List to get a text alert

with news about New Releases, Giveaways, Bargains and
Free books from Willow.

Cover design by Juan Villar Padron,
https://www.juanjpadron.com

Special thanks to my editor Janell Parque
http://janellparque.blogspot.com/

**To be the first to hear about new releases and bargains from
Willow Rose, sign up below to be on the VIP List.** (I promise
not to share your email with anyone else, and I won't clutter
your inbox.)

- Go here to sign up to be on the VIP LIST :
http://readerlinks.com/l/415254

Tired of too many emails? Text the word: "willowrose" to
31996 to sign up to Willow's VIP text List to get a text alert

with news about New Releases, Giveaways, Bargains and Free books from Willow.

Made in the USA
Middletown, DE
21 August 2024

59514136R00191